How to Da

M000267430

How to Date!

Single Girls' Dating Manual

India Kang

YOUCAXTON PUBLICATIONS

OXFORD & SHREWSBURY

DEDICATION

Big thank-you to my husband, Sid. This book would not have been possible without your ongoing encouragement and continued support. Huge thank-you to my clients from all over the world; it is a privilege to work with you all. I wish for you much love, success and happiness.

And thank you to my local Costa Coffee for letting me sit for hours and hours at the corner table. The one right at the back on the right-hand side.

This book is for single girls everywhere. May each of you find your personal happily ever after.

Copyright © India Kang 2016

The Author asserts the moral right to
be identified as the author of this work.

ISBN 978-191117-511-7
Printed and bound in Great Britain.
Published by YouCaxton Publications 2015

All rights reserved. No part of this publication may be reproduced,
stored in a retrieval system, or transmitted in any form or by
any means, electronic, mechanical, photocopying, recording or
otherwise, without the prior permission of the publisher.

This book is sold subject to the condition that it shall not, by way of
trade or otherwise, be lent, resold, hired out or otherwise circulated
without the publisher's prior consent in any form of binding or cover
other than that in which it is published and without a similar condition
including this condition being imposed on the subsequent purchaser.

CONTENTS

INTRODUCTION

I bet you weren't taught how to date.

The fact is no one is ever taught how to date! The general assumption is that dating doesn't need to be taught, but rather, is picked up naturally. We're all expected to know.

I will also bet your parents' generation probably didn't date either. Even if they did, they didn't date according to today's *modus operandi*. I know mine didn't. And when it came to dating advice they were useless. My parents' marriage was actually arranged by the village elders. OK we're talking 1960's. The dating landscape has certainly changed a whole lot since then. Meeting eligible men at the local village dance hall is also a thing of the past.

The first think I want you to know is that, irrespective of your ethnic background, geographical location or culture, urban dating is tougher than ever. It doesn't matter if you live in New York, Hong Kong or the leafy villages in Surrey. Dating is work and it takes time to find Mr Right.

Your age and life stage don't make much of a difference either. Whether you're twenty and searching, thirty-nine and divorced, fifty and divorced with two children, or sixty and never married, you will each experience your own set of unique challenges. Whereas a twenty-year-old, perhaps due to a lack of experience with men, may struggle with trusting her own judgement, a sixty-year-old with the proliferation of dating sites and apps now available has to grapple with technology.

If you're finding dating tough and hard work - that's because it is. Sometimes a girl will get 'lucky'. She may meet her guy who becomes her husband whilst on a random night out. These types of stories do exist.

I have one client who met her guy two weeks after I created her online dating profile. They married. I have another client who met her guy while out dancing with friends. Her story was particularly heart-warming because she was divorced after a twenty-year marriage and single for ten years after her divorce. She was fifty years old when she finally met 'The One' and in her own words 'he was the love of her life'. Another client met her guy whilst taking the tube in to work. They also married. I have to add; these types of stories are the exception rather than the norm.

For the most part it's not unusual to date for many months and often years before meeting your personal Mr Right. It took me two years and many dates before I met my husband. He was worth the wait!

I started my search in 2010. And I once typed into Google 'what happens on a date'. I wanted specifics. I wasn't interested in general dating advice; I wanted someone to explain what happens on dates, who pays and why don't men call you back.

I too was once confused about dating – not surprising given my cultural background. After coaching hundreds and hundreds of singletons and many thousands online, I know that many of you are encountering the same confusion and pain points. I spend a lot of my time coaching clients and explaining that their dating experiences are absolutely 'normal'.

Whether you're looking for marriage; actively dating but having little or no luck; or perhaps you're new to the dating scene and need a little guidance – great news, you're in the right place.

Dating is a process. The chapters in this book are structured so as to take you from dating novice to dating pro. I'm going to show you exactly what to do and how to do it.

This book is a practical 'how to' guide that provides the necessary tools and resources to ease your dating journey - and ultimately assist your path to your personal happily ever after. Any examples or stories shared have been done (where possible) with my clients' consent and permission. My clients' privacy and confidentiality is my first priority and is of utmost important. Any references made to *The Rulesbook* by Ellen Fein and Sherrie Schneider is also with their consent. They were also both kind enough to endorse this book.

I'm not going to mess about too much with long-winded introductions, forewords or prefaces. I'm keeping things simple. So let's dive straight in.

I hope you find this book a useful resource and please come visit soon, either via my website indiakang.com, or via social media channels, or alternatively write via india@indiakang.com.

I look forward to hearing from you.

India Kang xx

PART ONE
THE PREPARATION

Become Who You Want to Date

I'm going to start at the very beginning and I'd like to apologise in advance if any of this comes across as direct.

In order to attract a great mate you have to become a great mate: you have to become who you want to date. Thankfully this doesn't mean you have to become a man. This means personally possessing the exact traits and attributes that you're looking to attract.

When it comes to dating we all have a Desirability Rating and everything begins with you.

A Desirability Rating is a type of 'score' which indicates how attractive and desirable you're perceived to be by the opposite sex.

A Desirability Rating isn't all about looks, although for men looks are important in the beginning, since men are visual creatures; they fall in love with their eyes. Being desirable to others is equally about your attitude, personality, temperament, character, manner, mind-set, vibe together with the right amount of *je ne sais quoi*.

Your position on the Desirability-Rating Scale isn't fixed. You can increase your rating by setting self-improvement goals which improve your overall 'attractiveness'. Most people are happy to stay exactly where they are on the Desirability Scale. You will only ever attract a long-term partner with a similar Desirability Rating as you.

It's unrealistic to want to attract a partner with a Desirability Rating of ten when you're only a five for example and vice versa.

Let me explain what I mean. I remember talking to a client. She was thirty-three, single and ready to meet Mr Right. Her main crib was her weight. She felt overweight. She aspired to wear a UK dress size eight but confessed that she wasn't prepared to do the work involved. She was currently a UK size sixteen.

I asked 'What are you looking for?'

I hoped she wouldn't say 'someone who is honed and toned'.

She responded, 'Someone who is overweight is good enough for me, after all I have to look at myself first.'

What struck me about her and the reason she's remained lodged in my memory was - she was realistic. She didn't fantasise about meeting a body-builder. She knew she wasn't perfect and wasn't looking to attract perfection either.

This may sound odd because surely we're all aware of our imperfections. Not always, and unfortunately, after talking to hundreds of you, some singletons do suffer from a small dose of unrealism. This tiny spoonful of unrealism regrettably keeps them single.

I recall another client who was forty years old and would only date younger men. She wasn't prepared to date anyone older or in her own age group. She couldn't find what she was looking for. Another client who was fifty-two became upset when men in their sixties started writing to her online. She couldn't believe the types of men she was attracting and she stopped dating. She now refuses to date.

Sadly, you can't sit on the sofa, watch TV all day, rarely venture out, rarely exercise and expect to attract an adventurous, sporty guy.

Why?

Like attracts like.

Here's a quick exercise to work out if what you're looking for is realistic.

- Write a list outlining what you want in a potential mate.

- Now make a list of all your best qualities including what you can offer a potential mate. I'm going to guess you're looking for a great guy. No doubt there are certain attributes he must possess in order to qualify as your Mr Right. In the same way there are certain attributes Mr Right wants from you too.

- Now look at the two lists. Do they match? For example, if you're searching for a mate who enjoys sports and is a high flyer makes sure you share the same attributes. If you do - great.

If there is a disparity between what you want versus what you can offer I can provide two solutions either:

a. **Change what you're looking for and make it more realistic.** Maybe consider lowering your expectations a little. You never know who you may attract. Otherwise, if you want to attract high flyer types, find out where they hang out and start frequenting these places regularly, maybe try and seek employment in a FTSE top-100 company or attend professional balls. In short go to where these types of men spend their time

b. **Self-improve and work on increasing your date-ability.** If you're looking to attract high-profile professional types, maybe consider going back to school and working on your own skills and qualifications. Or perhaps you're shy with a small group of friends yet you want to meet someone who is social with a large network of friends. You know what to do.

If you want to attract better quality partners, aim to raise your Desirability Rating.

The other thing to add up-front is that dating isn't therapy. No man can 'fix' you. No man can erase your past pains. No man can fulfil all your physical, social, emotional and spiritual needs.

This is up to you to solve. The good news is that you're in charge of your own happiness.

Don't expect love will conquer all either. This is a slight fallacy. Don't assume that, if he loves you, he'll put up with your struggles. No one wants to invest in a liability. Yes, he'll be sympathetic and understanding - provided you're taking responsibility for resolving your own issues and affairs.

Does this mean: if you have baggage (who doesn't) you won't meet anyone?

No, the point is to take responsibility for your own baggage. Don't let any struggles or past hurts become a permanent feature in your relationship.

Doesn't he deserve the best you?

Don't you deserve the best you?

Your job in the beginning is to become the best you possible.

Set Your Intentions

Intention is the starting point of every desire. If you've never set any relationship intentions, now is an excellent time to start since everything that happens in the universe begins with intention.

The ideal time to set your intentions is while in a meditative state. I'm fairly new to meditation, but if you're a pro then be sure to set your intentions while meditating.

Maybe you already know all about setting your intentions. If you don't here's another little exercise I set my clients.

All you have to do is verbalise your intentions and let go of the outcome. Say your intentions out loud. It's best if you're home alone when doing this otherwise your flatmate, or family if you live at home, might dial the asylum. I used to verbalise my intentions while standing in front of the bathroom mirror. One day my flatmate knocked on the bathroom door to ask who I was talking to and whether I was ok.

I said, 'yes, give me a second, be right out. I'm setting my intentions.'

Here's one of the many intentions I set:

'I want to meet and marry in one year under grace and in a perfect way'.

If you're new to setting intentions there is plenty out there to help you. To start you off, Florence Scovel Shinn's book, *The Game of Life and How to Play It*, is excellent and a great resource.

According to Florence, you have to ask right. If you don't have time to read her book, she says that best way to ask right is to add the words 'under grace and in perfect ways' after each of your intentions.

Go ahead and set your intentions! Once set and released, detach from the outcome and let the Universe handle the details.

The Vision Board

A vision board is another useful visualization tool, mainly because our minds respond strongly to visual stimulation. If you already know your dreams, now is a good time to illustrate them visually.

Creating a vision board is easy. If you've never created a vision board, here's how to do it. If you want to create a vision board digitally there are apps which will help you do this. A quick Google will help identify which apps are currently available.

Start with the Pictures

Find the necessary imagery. Most imagery is available free. Use whatever imagery is available; you can use photographs, magazine cut-outs, or you can simply download online. Basically, use whatever inspires you. The images must represent or symbolize the experiences, feelings and possessions you want to attract into your life; they must make you feel good or spark joy.

Place the images on your board. You can also post affirmations, inspirational words, quotations, and thoughts. Again, choose words and images that inspire you and make you feel good.

Keep it simple and neat and really think about the images you select to place on your vision board. Try not to create a cluttered or chaotic board. You don't want to attract clutter into your life.

Don't stop at only one vision board. You can create multiple vision boards, for example, one for your relationships and another for personal and career goals.

Using Your Vision Board.

Once created, print out your vision board in colour and pin it somewhere where you can see it daily. If you have a digital vision board, maybe make it your screen saver. Spend time each morning and evening visualizing, affirming, believing and internalizing your goals.

You can update your vision board at any point. Maybe start each year or even each quarter with a new vision board. There are no limits. Remember, what the mind perceives can be achieved.

Don't take forever creating a vision board. I created mine one afternoon; it's digital and it took me half a day. It may take you longer but it shouldn't take months.

Go ahead, put this book down, set your intentions and create your vision board.

Decluttering

You may wonder what decluttering has to do with dating and relationships. When I tell my clients that decluttering will help to achieve success in their relationships, I'm typically met with some scepticism.

Clutter and unwanted stuff in our lives including unwanted relationships strangles our *joie de vivre*.

Here are two ways you can declutter.

Declutter Your Physical Space

Before we begin sorting your dating outfits and getting you date-ready, now is an opportune time to have a little clear-out. It's incredible how a little clear-out can rejuvenate one's spirits.

I always considered myself a good declutterer. I regularly sorted through wardrobes and cupboards and would deposit bags at the local charity shop. After every decluttering session I always felt lighter. Then I read an incredible book titled *The Life-Changing Magic of Tidying: A Simple, Effective Way to Banish Clutter Forever* by Marie Kondo.

I thought I was big on decluttering, but this book took decluttering to whole new level. In a nutshell, the method described in the book is about changing your relationship with the stuff you own. The basic concept is to only surround yourself with things that spark joy – you decide what you want to keep, not necessarily what you want to throw away.

Make sure you declutter all the physical space you spend your time in on a regular basis: typically your home, workspace and even your car.

I encourage you to read this book and watch the magic of tidying transform your mind-set. Don't believe me? - try it!

Declutter Your Relationships

It might feel a little unnatural to talk about decluttering your relationships like you would do your belongings, but similar rules apply. We're all directly influenced by the people we surround ourselves with. To declutter your relationships, you need to be around people who love and support you. When it comes to relationships the rule is simple: 'love those who love you'. You will already know the people who love you. Spend time with these types of people. The same principles apply when dating: we're only interested in men who move towards you and are trying to take you out. There's no point wasting time on men who don't want you.

Male Visual Cues

Now that you've set your intentions, created your vision board and decluttered let's talk about what men find visually appealing.

In case you didn't already know men and women are different.

We're actually very different. We're both part of the *Homo Sapiens* race but from a biological, evolutionary and chemical point of view - we're different.

Simply put: we're wired differently.

A man's primary role was to hunt. If he didn't hunt and bring back food our ancestors might have starved which means you probably wouldn't be reading this book now.

Comparing men to women is a little like comparing apples and oranges. Apples and oranges are both classified as fruits yet they taste and smell different. They provide different nutrients and are packaged differently.

The skin of an apple is edible whereas orange rind which can be used for cooking is bitter and is often discarded. To get angry because men are visual and respond to certain visual cues is parallel to getting angry with the weather for being the weather.

Don't get mad; get smart! Once you understand why men respond to the cues they do, you can adapt. There's little point in fighting his wiring.

From a visual point of view men tend to use physical attributes as a way to gauge women's attractiveness and to find potential mates. Here's what men respond to and why;

- Long hair - hair denotes fertility. Yes, as simple as that.

- Dangly earrings or hoops earrings – the ears are associated with sensuality.

- Heels – elongate the leg and change a woman's gait which men find attractive.

- Bright colours – Most men are colour-blind and tend to wear grey, black and blue. Again it's evolutionary. Men were hunters, wearing bright clothes would alert their prey. That said men love colour on women.

- Good general grooming - Men are attracted to women who look healthy because health makes women good gene carriers.

If you're serious about meeting the one, get smart. Dress for men. Wear clothes that flatter, show off and accentuate your figure.

Why?

Dress for men because it's MEN you want to attract.

Isn't it about what's on the inside?

Not in the beginning, sorry.

He can't get to the inside unless he likes what he sees on the outside. It's the way it is, just like the weather.

The great news is that you can cheat a little in lots of ways. Here are a few cheats although I'm sure you can think of a few more.

- Make-up cleverly applied

- Hair extensions

- False lashes

- Healthy and well-groomed nails

- Well-fitted clothes which hide your bad bits and accentuate your good bits

- Eating well

- Exercise

- Spanx

Doing all the things you love only add to your glow.

Little bits of sorcery never hurt anyone.

If you smoke or drink alcohol heavily now may be a good time to quit. I've never come across a man who wants to meet someone who is 'overweight, smokes and drinks too much!'

If you smoke and are looking to quit, the best advice I can give you is to try Allen Carr's *Easy Way to Stop Smoking*. There are many other ways to quit including hypnotherapy, the will-power method, lifestyle changes, nicotine patches. Find what works for you.

If you're drinking too much alcohol try Allen Carr's *Easy Way to Control Drinking*. Again there are many other ways to reduce your alcohol intake. Allen Carr's books have made a positive difference to many of my clients' lives, which is why I'm recommending them here.

If you're overweight and want to lose weight, and based purely on what's worked for the majority of my clients, I would suggest you try joining a slimming club. Once again, there are many other ways to control your weight including working with a nutritionist, or following a particular exercise and eating plan. This isn't a book on diet and nutrition. I'm simply sharing what's worked for the majority of my clients in the hope it may work for you.

Get Date-Ready and Organised

Every project requires preparation. And your love life needs a little preparation too.

Maybe you're thinking your love life isn't a project?

Well, your love life is really no different to any other part of your life. There are courses that show you how to 'build your career' or 'how to invest wisely'; you can take courses on just about anything and everything. If you aspire to work in a particular profession, let's say medicine, undoubtedly you will need many years of study followed by exams. All of this before you can even start to practise medicine let alone open up your own surgery.

Yet often when it comes to their love life, many people falsely assume: 'It will just happen.' Holding this false assumption will probably keep you single.

Yes, now and again a girl will meet a great guy. She will indeed explain, 'it just happened.' These stories, whilst real, are very much in the minority. For the vast majority of singletons, including me, you have to do the work.

There's a popular saying: 'Marriages are made in heaven and ordained on earth'. My culture has its own version of the same saying. Whoever said this failed to add that here on earth you have to make it happen.

I really don't know whether marriages are made in heaven and ordained on earth but I do know that if you want to meet Mr Right you really have to take positive, consistent and persistent steps to date. Please don't think that one day Mr Right will fall out of the sky and simply land on your lap. He might, however on the whole, just like every other aspect of your life, it requires some effort and work on your part.

Last year I was talking to a lovely client, she was forty-six, never married and single. She had a couple of bad dates and proclaimed, 'That's it; I'm off men for the rest of the year. I'm no longer going to search.'

'Really?' I quizzed.

'Well,' she said, 'I'm no longer searching but if a great guy happens to come along, well, that's different.'

This is another tactic or way of thinking that will keep you single. What she was really saying was:

'Ok, I admit I want to meet a great guy but I don't want to do the work involved. So I'll just stop looking because it's way easier than having to date. It sure feels better not to have to think about dating. Maybe if I stop looking and making an effort I'll get lucky and meet someone.'

Which is a little like saying, 'I want to find a new job but I can't be bothered to look or show up for interviews.'

Sure, but be prepared to stay unemployed.

If you're serious about dating and finding a committed and rewarding relationship, we have some work to do. Don't leave your dating life to chance.

One of the first things I want you to do is get yourself ready to date. This requires taking some practical steps which will help ease your dating journey.

Please remember, dating is no different to any other part of your life. Anyone looking for a job would invest in a new suit or a new dress. You're unlikely to attend an interview wearing jeans; chances are you would dress accordingly and ensure that your shoes were polished. Dating works in the same way.

Firstly I'd like you to organise your wardrobe. We're going to work out your dating outfits.

Empty out your closets. We've already talked about decluttering. Once emptied, we're going to pre-plan your dating outfits, for the first few dates only, and this is how we're going to do it:

- Work out your date zero, date one, date two outfits only.

These are the actual clothes you're going to wear on dates. You can wear the same outfit for all your date zeros, dates one and dates two. You only need one outfit because you will only ever have one date zero and one date one with the same guy. He will only ever see your outfit once. If he progresses to a date two, then he will only see your date two outfit once too. So lots of men will see the same outfit - but only once. The reason we're only organising outfits for the first few dates is because most of your dates will be dates zero or dates one. You will have lots and lots of dates zero and dates one. This is normal and we'll talk more about it later.

Don't worry if you don't know what a date zero is yet. We'll come to that shortly.

Back to clothes and let me give you an example. For my date zeros I used to wear white or blue city-type shorts, a pink sequinned round-necked top and a jacket. If it was cold, I'd wear tights underneath my shorts and introduce a thicker jacket to wear over my top. If the weather was hot, I would simply ditch the tights and the jacket. When organising your outfits, consider the weather for your region. It may take some time to work out your outfits. When buying any new clothes, I would often think in terms of 'are these appropriate for dates'. This is probably why I was able to organise my dating outfits in one day: I already had enough date-appropriate clothes.

- Check you have the appropriate underwear and hosiery for each outfit.

Invest in some Spanx; you can never have too much. Buy as much as you need in black and nude, different types for different occasions. Also invest in some nude underwear. You can't go wrong with nude-coloured bras and knickers.

If you haven't already done so, get your bra size measured properly and invest in some good quality bras. You need nude and black as a minimum. Make sure you have strapless bras. You can buy coloured underwear too but for the purposes of practicality, you will find nude and black underwear are multi-purpose and work with a myriad of outfits. Knowing you have the appropriate underwear will prevent any last minute running around. Same with hosiery: make sure it is clean and ready to wear within a minute's notice.

- Check you have the right accessories which includes jewellery, shoes, bags etc.

Make sure your accessories match your outfits or vice versa. Get your shoes re-heeled if necessary and store them in shoe bags or boxes. Don't wear worn-out shoes on dates. As you know you need heels - invest in some new ones. A pair of nude-coloured heels are a winner. I purchased mine from Kurt Geiger and they are the most hard-working pair of shoes ever. They literally work with any outfit.

- Do a recce on your make up including any and all products.

Go through all your products including make-up, make-up brushes together with any other products you use on a regular basis, for example: make-up removers, cleansing wipes, toners, moisturisers, face masks, hair masks, deodorants, perfumes etc. Bin old make-up that has passed its sell-by date and wash all your brushes or anything that you use to apply your make-up.

Once you've done all of this, invest in some decent hangers. Organise your entire dating outfits on hangers and hang them 'ready' in your wardrobe. Now, if you have a date, all you need to do is pull out the relevant outfit, pop it on - and off you go.

You can of course change your outfits as many times as you want. If you prefer to wear a different outfit for each and every date, please do so.

I found that organising my outfits in this way meant there was one less thing to consider when heading out on a date. No longer did I have to worry about 'what to wear' and I was never caught short; for example, I never ran out of make-up or hair spray because I had prepared in advance.

I'm assuming you have enough clothes in your wardrobe that are date-appropriate and that make you feel good. If not, it's time to go shopping. Either go alone or take someone you trust. Maybe consider booking a session with a personal shopper, some of the major department stores offer free personal shopping. While you're out shopping, stock up on extra make-up, any products that you use regularly. Sometimes it helps to have duplicates of the same products so you can leave some make-up at work, ready and prepared for any lunch or after-work dates. I would also recommend leaving a pair of heels, toiletries and a nice top at work too.

If all of this already sounds like too much work, you can organise for a wardrobe makeover. There are professionals who will come into your home and help organise your wardrobes. Maybe also consider a session with an image consultant; they'll help you work out which colours and shapes suit you best. Remember to try to wear colour on your dates because, as specified, men love colour.

Let's have a quick recap: grow your hair or consider getting some extensions and make sure you get your nails done. Men love long hair and they always notice your nails. Good grooming tells men you care about yourself, which means that you'll care about your relationships too.

I did all of the above while dating. It made life easier because I was no longer stressing over what to wear because I already knew. Neither are you caught short because you've run out of deodorant; you're prepared! Aren't we the smarty cats?

Don't forget to wash or dry-clean your outfits in between dates.

Create a Dating Strategy

I was once asked if men knew I had a dating strategy. Probably not, I would have thought. It was never something I shared on dates. I guess the word 'strategy' conjures images of game-playing or manipulation, but strategy in this context means 'to plan' or take active, consistent and persistent steps to meet men.

Having a dating strategy is no different to having a career strategy or a saving plan. A saving plan helps you work out how much you can afford to save each month. With a career plan you work out where you want to be and how you're going to get there. A dating strategy works in exactly the same way.

What I'm saying is: don't leave your love life to chance.

Get smart! And here's how:

Print off a monthly calendar or maybe use your diary or journal. Work out everything you're going to do to meet suitable, eligible men. Your individual circumstances will determine the required level of action. For example, if you're over thirty-five, never married, and want to start a family you should take anything between three to four social actions a week to meet men. Some of these actions could include online dating, mobile dating apps, and attending single meet-ups. Basically use as many channels as possible to meet suitable men. If you're forty-one, never married, and also want to start a family, you have even less time to waste. I would encourage you to take anything between four and five social actions a week to meet men. The more the better.

If you're fifty, with children and divorced. The biological clock isn't ticking so loudly; you can take two social actions per week to meet men.

Social actions can include anything from after-work drinks with colleagues to sitting in a coffee shop by yourself dressed up with your make-up on. I once saw an article in *The New York Times* about single girls dressing up and hanging out in the financial districts. Smart. You really have to go to where the men are. How on earth are they supposed to find you otherwise?

Once your dating strategy is complete. Monitor the results every quarter, or monthly if necessary, and change tactics accordingly. For example, if attending salsa classes is one of your social actions but the room is full of women, you might be better off exchanging salsa for maybe the golf club.

Another little technique is to begin each week with a weekly dating schedule.

A typical sample week may look something like this:

Monday	Gym
Tuesday	Check online dating sites and mobile dating sites
Wednesday	Free day
Thursday	Check online dating sites and mobile dating sites
Friday	Out with friends
Saturday	Speed dating
Sunday	Check online dating sites and mobile apps

I suggest you get into the habit of checking online dating sites and apps three times a week. The days to check are Tuesdays, Thursdays and Sundays. That way you date and still have a life.

And you can scale the activity up and down accordingly. Let's say, one week lots of men ask you for dates. That week you can probably miss the speed-dating on Saturday since you have enough 'potentials' that week. Conversely, if it's a slow week, increase your dating actions.

This may sound like a lot but it's not. You have to treat dating like a full time job.

I bet you easily spend an hour or more a day checking social media sites like Facebook, Twitter or Instagram; divert that time and energy into dating. I'm not suggesting you stay online for hours and hours, no, not at all. In fact, I suggest you log onto your dating sites and stay online for thirty minutes to one-hour maximum per session.

The time you spend online depends on how many messages you get. If you only get a few messages, you can log off fairly quickly. Bear in mind that every week will produce different results. If you manage your dating life this way, it's very possible to work full time, date and still have a life. I know because I did it too. My background is in advertising - very long hours.

On Tuesdays, Thursdays and Sundays my dinner was often a simple affair such as soup or a quick, ready meal. Sometimes I would eat dinner while checking messages online.

What if you work long hours? I have one client with a heavy workload. She once went for a date and then went back to work. She was working on a huge project. She left her office at 6pm, had a quick drink date and then went back to work. It is possible providing you're willing to be flexible a little.

The point is to get organised and get smart. You don't have to keep this schedule forever. It's only until you meet Mr Right. It's simply a means to an end.

Safety First

When it comes to dating, safety is absolutely paramount. Please don't take any risks. I recall once sharing these tips which I'm sharing with you now on a radio show and the radio host laughed. I couldn't understand why she laughed because when dating you're effectively meeting strangers.

I'm sure you're already familiar with what I'm about to say. In case you're not. Here are some dating safety tips:

Create a Separate Email Address for Dating.

This becomes your dating email. It's a completely separate email account which is solely for dating purposes.

Don't create a silly email address like lookingforhusband@gmail.com or misssexy@gmail.com. I don't think you would but no harm in reminding you.

Don't disclose your full name either, especially if you have an unusual name or if you're in the public eye. For example, if your name is Melissa Brown your dating email could be melb@gmail.com or if that's not available you could try melb11@gmail.com. That way you keep your privacy. In the beginning keep your personal details private.

Avoid using your age for example melb33@gmail.com because what happens when you turn thirty-four?

Don't use the year either for example melb2016@gmail.com because again what happens if you're still dating in two years' time.

Dating Phone

Another great safety feature is to get yourself a dating phone.

There are apps and services like Google voice, which are available and will do the job. Otherwise simply buy a cheap pay-as-you-go phone. If you already have a handset, buy a sim. The additional media or fancy data isn't necessary. All you need is the ability to make and receive calls and texts. A pay-as-you-go phone has an added security bonus - there's no need to register the phone. Another great way to keep your details private.

The other merit of a dating phone is that you can easily change your number should anyone become a nuisance. Extra protection from stalkers and booty calls. Turn your phone off at night and sleep peacefully, knowing that anyone important who needs to urgently make contact already has your private number. Ingenious and simple, all at the same time. Aren't we smarty cats?

Sometimes when I tell clients to get a dating phone, I'm met with some resistance. In case you're feeling some resistance - here are my responses to some commonly asked questions about the dating phone.

So I have to carry two phones with me?
Yes, you can do it; phones are small.

I already have two phones. I have a work and business phone and now you're saying to get another phone?
You're already used to carrying two phones; one more won't make much difference, clever, smart, multi-tasker you!!

Won't he think I'm a player?
No, he'll think you're smart. If he's smart he'll already have a dating phone. Some men take their privacy seriously. Men don't want stalkers or bunny boilers either.

If we end up becoming boyfriend and girlfriend, how do I give him my real number?

Easy, when the time's right very playfully say something like: 'Well then Adam - today is your lucky day, today I'm upgrading you to my private number' and then giggle.

He'll laugh. Then give him your private number. The above is exactly what I did with my husband. He was impressed that I took my security seriously.

A dating phone saves time and headaches too. With a separate dating phone any crazies can be safely blocked. I know this doesn't always stop them; sometimes they call using another number or write with a different email address.

If you do get a stalker your safety isn't compromised. Simply get rid of the phone and get another one. Meanwhile all your personal contacts remain intact. Less stress and drama.

Finally, a dating phone stops exes or old flames making contact when you're happily exclusive with your guy. Sometimes men call out of the blue. Either he's bored, still single, or he's remembering you and thinks 'emm she was OK, wonder if she's still single, maybe I'll try her'. Maybe he's going through a break-up and trying to access his options. It's unfortunate his timing is off because you've long moved on. Once engaged or married, you can delete your dating email and ditch the dating phone. The last thing you want is for the ex to make contact while you're snuggled in bed next to your fiancé.

I hope I've made a good case. Please be savvy, invest in a dating phone and don't complain about having to carry two phones. I know you won't.

Google Your Date and While You're at it Google Yourself Too.

Google yourself first and no this doesn't make you vain; it's smart. He will probably Google you anyway.

Why wouldn't he?

Google yourself so you can see what he will see. If there's something you don't like, try and get it removed. I'm really not sure how to do that but Google it.

Google him but don't tell him. Whatever you find out about him via the internet or via his social media, keep it to yourself. All of it. There's no need to tell him you Googled him and found out x and y. Some experts tell you to never Google your dates but I'm the opposite. I used to Google my dates whenever possible, check out their LinkedIn profiles, the whole kit and caboodle, anonymously of course. In my opinion it's no different to Googling a prospective employer prior to a job interview.

Always Meet in Busy Places

If you're meeting for a quick coffee or drink date, don't go to secluded places. No bars or restaurants situated in dark alleys. For evening dates, again, meet in busy areas with lots of people.

Always Tell Someone Where You're Going

Always safety first. I used to tell my flatmate. You may or may not have a flatmate, in which case tell a close friend. If you live at home, you could tell your parents, providing they're not going to give you the Spanish inquisition when you get back. If they're likely to quiz you, it might be easier and less hassle to tell a friend or a chilled relative instead. In either case, find someone and make sure they know where you are.

Never Go Back to his Place

I don't think this requires any further explanation. Never ever go back to his place. Not in the beginning. If he needs to go back to his place to pick something up, wait outside, smile sweetly and tell him 'oh you go, I'll wait here.'

Never Invite Him Into Your Place

Another no-brainer although allow me to expand a little.

Sometimes men will want to pick you up for dates. In this instance there are two options:

- If you don't feel safe, meet him in a location convenient for you, for example outside a tube station if you live in a city

- Conversely meet near a key landmark. Again somewhere convenient for you. Ordinarily I'd meet my dates outside the nearest tube station either Parson's Green or Fulham Broadway. I would sometimes meet my dates outside the wine shop on the high street. The wine shop was called Nicolas and was located on Fulham High Road. That's where I met a couple of my dates. No one ever blinked or made any comments. Even if they did, I didn't care; I felt safer meeting on a busy high street.

You Don't Have to Give Him Your Address

No you don't. As mentioned above, meet near a key landmark somewhere convenient for you and preferably somewhere busy.

Should You Get Into His Car?

If you don't know him, don't get into his car. If he's driving to you and wants to pick you up but you don't feel safe, as mentioned, tell him to meet somewhere nearby. Always safety first.

My husband actually picked me up from outside my flat. In my husband's case I felt safe enough to get into his car. We'd spoken on the phone a couple of times before we met and I discovered we had family in common; his childhood friend Jas is married to my cousin Harvey. Small world right? The only reason I let him pick me up is because he came pre-screened.

You can also turn down offers to be driven home. If he's coming to you, your journey home shouldn't take long anyway. If he insists, tell him 'thank you but I'm ok getting back.'

PART TWO
THE WORK

Do the Work

Dating isn't easy; incidentally, neither is marriage. Both require work, effort, a huge dose of realism and a degree of maturity on your part as well as your partner's. If you're finding dating tough that's because it *is* tough.

You have to do the work and I fully realise this is an ongoing theme. Rather than resisting, I'm going to encourage you to surrender to the effort.

Perhaps you've tried all the easy and obvious approaches, but the goal simply won't succumb; don't give up just because your previous twenty dates didn't work out. You may need to make hundreds of attempts, not necessarily because your goal requires so much experimentation but because you need all that training to become strong enough to succeed.

Embrace the required work; drop the unnecessary resistance. Some goals are far more difficult than you first imagined.

One way to shift your mind-set is to read a great book called *Do The Work* by Steven Pressfield; I recommend you get a copy. After reading his book I myself decided to 'do the work'. I concluded, no matter how I looked at things, the work had to get done and the only person who could do it was me! You're in charge of your love life and it's not a case of 'what will be will be;' it's a case of 'it will happen when you take charge'.

What does 'doing the work' mean?

It means: commit to finding Mr Right and don't give up until you've met your personal Mr Right. Yes, there will be times when things are slow, but keep going through these times and decide to never, ever give up. And don't be upset by the results you didn't get because of the work you didn't do.

Don't give up at the first hurdle, or at the first disappointment; there will be plenty of both. The best advice I can give is to 'get on with it'. I appreciate this may not be exactly what you want to hear; sorry, it's the truth.

I can guarantee you will have your fair share of dating highs and low. My aim is to show you that your experiences are mostly normal. To date and not expect disappointment is like expecting life to be fair. Life isn't fair and dating is work.

That said, it's not all doom and gloom. Dating *does* work. By this I mean that by dating you will get results and by results you will meet your personal Mr Right.

If you're dating several years and still searching, firstly - get in touch. Whenever I hear this and probe a little deeper, I find there is always a reason and often two which will explain your single status.

One of the best things you can do in your search for Mr Right, is to find your passion.

Finding your passion makes dating a hellavalot easier. There's little time to worry about men who don't call back because you're so busy working on your passion. You may even be grateful for any no-shows because that allows more time to work on what you love.

Here are some quick tips to help you find your passion;

- It's ok to try out lots of different passions before deciding on your final passion.

- You know when you've found your true passion because it feels like play.

- Another way of knowing your calling is because time flies when you're working on it.

- Your passion may not give you financial rewards straight away but there are some things money can't buy.

- You don't need lots of money to start your passion and don't assume you need fancy equipment or plush offices. I'm currently writing this book in a coffee shop.

- Unfortunately, some people will pass this lifetime without ever finding their passion.

- Adverse circumstances can work for your good. Often when we're down on our luck this creates new opportunities and a great breeding-ground for growth.

- Make a start and don't worry about making it perfect. You can perfect as you go.

How Much Should You Date?

I'm often asked this question. The answer depends on your personal circumstances including your age and what you're looking for, together with how loud the biological clock is ticking.

As already specified, anyone aged late thirties to early forties who wants to start a family, should take as much action to meet men as humanly possible. Subscribe to every single dating site and dating app. Attend singles events two or three times a week if not every day. And I'm not exaggerating; this is the level of action required to even give yourself a chance of meeting Mr Right.

If you're in your early twenties and not looking for marriage, you can ease up a little. If you're in your early thirties, take two or three social actions a week to meet men. If you're aged over fifty, again, take two or three actions a week.

How many dates per week will guarantee success? This is a little harder to quantify and it's difficult to predict how many dating actions will result in actual dates. Sometimes this will be zero, other times this may lead to two or three dates. It's futile to try and aim for three dates a week as it doesn't work that way. It's similar to job hunting and aiming for three interviews a week; some weeks you may have five interviews, other weeks you may have zilch. Each week is different. One thing is for sure: if you're low on dates, take more action.

Working with my many wonderful clients, I can tell you that the majority of singles don't take enough action to meet men, not by a long shot! Most girls underestimate the level of work required to meet Mr Right.

If in doubt take more not less action.

Beliefs That Sabotage Your Success

Changing your mind-set and removing false beliefs is paramount to your dating success. If you've ever heard any of the statements below, I want you to know that they are all complete baloney. Here's what I mean by false beliefs:

- It'll happen when it will happen

- It'll happen when you're not looking for it

- You don't know what's around the corner

- Maybe you're trying too hard; just relax

- Maybe it won't happen for me

- Maybe I'm destined to stay single

- It's too late for me

- What will be will be. I'm going to continue living my life and whatever's meant to happen will

All of the above are phony. These statements are nonsense and are often voiced by you, close friends, family and loved ones. Some are aired to make you feel better and, admittedly, they do provide momentarily relief but that's about all - since you're still single!

Let's dispel each one in turn. Are you ready? Here we go.

It will happen when it will happen
No it will happen when YOU decide to make it happen.

It'll happen when you're not looking for it
Possibly, but not likely. It'll happen when you actively search and take consistent, persistent steps to meet men.

You don't know what's around the corner
Yes, you do. There's a bend around the corner.

Maybe you're trying too hard; just relax
No, try harder. In my experience most girls don't undertake the required work to meet men. Do as much as you possibly can to meet men. It's almost impossible to take too many actions to meet men.

Maybe it won't happen for me
Only if you say so.

Maybe I'm destined to stay single
I was once told by a palmist friend that we can change our destinies. He explained that the lines on our non-active hand (often the left as most people are right handed) remain stagnant; the lines on our active hand (usually our right hand) change according to our actions. He explained that we all have the tools to change our destinies. If you believe you're destined to stay single – you will.
I don't believe you're destined to stay single. They say success is a system. I haven't cracked the 'success' system but I've made huge inroads to cracking the dating system. With the right tools and the right mind-set, you can win the dating game.

36

It's too late for me

It's never too late. You can meet Mr Right at any age. I heard a story of a couple who met when they were in their eighties, a true story. They met and married. It's not over until it's over.

What will be will be, I'm just going to carry on living my life and if it's meant to happen it will

It will happen when you decide to make it happen. And, as already explained, you can still have a life and date. Dating doesn't halt your life; if anything it will enhance your life. Hopefully you'll meet a great guy who will add to your life. By all means live your life but also date and it can be done. Yes, it does take work and some preparation. I can tell you that the rewards are worth the effort.

Things You Should Get Used to Very Quickly

I realise I'm constantly using 'work' as an analogy and I hope you don't mind the repetition. It's a simple and quick way to illustrate certain dating scenarios since nearly everyone can identify with work.

You don't mind?

Great because here it is again.

Dating is really no different to looking for a job. Anyone looking for work will undoubtedly start by updating their CV. Once the CV is updated, the search for jobs which match your work experience begins. There are many ways to search for a job: a couple of options are to enlist the help of recruitment agencies, or apply direct. Whichever channel you use it doesn't matter as long as you apply for the post.

Next there's a wait to see whether they think you're right for the role and, if so, it's onto the interview stage. Prior to the interview, if you're sensible you will read up on the company, practise answers to any difficult questions and organise your interview outfits. Getting the job offer is out of your control; you can't force them to give you the post. All you can do is your part.

Dating works in exactly the same way and I want you to shift your mind-set to start seeing dating for what it is – a process. Your job is to dress up, go to where the men are, turn up even though most of the time you probably won't feel like it - and release the outcome.

Some parts of the dating process, while super-infuriating and annoying, are completely standard. For some reason girls get into a real tizz if a date cancels or if he turns up without a date plan. They see it as a personal attack or as a reflection on their own self-worth. They feel a man should never cancel a date and, if he does, this somehow reflects on them. They start feeling there's something wrong with them. Well, if you're one of these types - there's nothing wrong with you. Sorry to be direct and forgive me but unfortunately the world doesn't revolve around you. Men are sometimes late. Don't take it personally because it's not personal.

Providing you're doing your part. All of the below scenarios, which women all over the world are grappling with, are normal and standard.

I guarantee you will experience some, if not all, of these scenarios and I want you to know it's just the way it is. Let's run through some of these very normal dating scenarios now – and if you haven't experienced any of these scenarios, you're not dating enough!

Majority of Your Dates Won't Make it Past the First Date

If this is happening to you, I can tell you this is standard. If this hasn't happened to you yet, it will. Only a small number and I'm talking single digits, for example maybe two or three men if you're lucky will make it past the first date. The remainder will fall. Very typical. The quicker you get used to this and accept it as part of the dating journey the better.

If you start accepting this truth right now, you'll save a lot of doubts such as: 'is there something wrong with me?' or 'aren't I pretty enough?' or 'am I doing something wrong?' You're doing nothing wrong - 99% of your dates won't make it past the first date. Either he won't call back or you won't like him.

Think about it this way: Mr Right is a special human being, perhaps unique, so most guys will not/cannot be your Mr Right.

Mr Right comes along maybe two, three or four times in a lifetime. Think about how often you find your dream job or dream house to use another example. The answer is: not often. Most people are very lucky to find their dream job in this lifetime; they will pass this lifetime without ever finding their passion. Most men will fall into the category of 'Mr Not-So-Right', or 'Mr Maybe' or 'Mr Never-in-a-Million-Years'. Mr Right is a rare gem. If the majority of your dates don't make it past the first date, don't worry because every 'no' is bringing you one step closer to a 'yes'.

You Will Get Stood Up

Yes, you will. I got stood up and so will you. Again, the advice I can give is to please try and accept it. It's a little like turning up for an interview only to be told the person who is meant to interview you, got called into an urgent meeting and can you please come back?

OK not quite the same thing but you get the idea. If you're constantly getting stood up, there's something wrong and we should talk, otherwise, no dating journey would be complete without a couple of men standing you up here and there. I would encourage you to make peace with this and accept it as simply your turn to 'get stood up'. Tomorrow it will be someone else's turn. It had to happen sooner or later. Move on quick and try not to dwell on it.

Men Will Arrive Late

They will. The majority of my dates arrived between forty and forty-five minutes late. Sure some were on time but the vast majority were late. There was one exception - my husband. He was either early or arrived on time. For our date zero he actually called to say 'he was ten minutes away'. Very thoughtful and extremely rare! How did I know this was rare and thoughtful? I had dated and dated and built up a huge repository of data. I would encourage you do the same and date 'wide.' That way, when a great guy comes along your dating antennaes are poised and alert.

What can you do if your date is late? Roll with it and take a good book.

Am I telling you to deal with it? Yes, that's exactly what I'm suggesting. Getting mad or angry won't get you anywhere; it simply raises your cortisol levels. When I was dating I lived in London. Sometimes dates would get lost on the underground; men travelling by car would underestimate the traffic or they wouldn't be able to find a parking space. What did I do? Waited and read my book. I used to think, 'oh goody maybe I can quickly finish this chapter'.

It helps to take something uplifting and energising to read. Load your Kindle or e-book reader with uplifting, fun and inspirational books and wait away. At least you haven't wasted any time.

Should you reprimand him? No, he may or may not apologise. Reprimanding him will only set a bad tone and you don't want to start the date frosty. Why didn't he call or text to say he was late? In my case sometimes he travelled by public transport and he couldn't because the London Underground doesn't have much of a phone signal. Sometimes they did, other times they didn't. I carried on reading.

Men Will Arrive Early

This is the same problem as men arriving early but in a different way. A couple of times in the early phases of dating my husband arrived early. The first time this happened he caught me out and I wasn't ready. It never happened again. I started to understand that he was an 'on time' or early type of guy. Once, while we were still dating, he was picking me up 2 pm one Saturday afternoon. He had planned an afternoon in Central London followed by an early-doors dinner. I was dressed and ready by 11 am. He'd already caught me out once and it wasn't going to happen again. I remember waking up that particular Saturday morning, going for an early morning run and once back from my run I started getting ready for my date. I remember thinking, 'I'm going to get showered and dressed and this way there's no panic; if he arrives early I'm ready'. Once date-ready I sat in my patio with a coffee, caught up with my flatmate and leisurely read the news. Now we're married and whenever we go anywhere we're always on time or early. What did I tell you? He's an 'arrive early' or 'always on time' type of guy.

What if you have a date and he calls to ask 'whether you can meet earlier?' or he calls to say that he's arrived early and is sitting in a local café waiting for you? Providing you're free, meet him. If you're at the theatre for example or at the gym , you won't be able to meet him. Chances are you might not see his message since your phone may be on silent or in the gym locker and, in this case, there's nothing you can do. If you're available and he says 'I'm here', provided it's convenient for you, go meet him.

Men Will Arrive Without a Date Plan

This was one of my biggest dating peeves. The majority of men would arrive without a date plan. I covered this scenario together with multiple others in my first book *Why Men Ask Dumb Dating Questions*. If you don't have a copy, let's run through this now:

One big reason a man may arrive without a date plan especially if he's travelling to you is because he doesn't know your area. He actually thinks it chivalrous to let you pick the date venue. But of course you don't pick; he picks because he's paying. It's only fair he gets to pick; let him pick and follow his lead. In any case, dating is not all about getting wined and dined at exclusive bars and restaurants; the brief is way bigger than a few fancy meals.

The brief at hand is your happily-ever-after. In the very early stages of dating, don't judge him for his choice of venue. Don't fret that he took you to a bar with tacky carpet and don't think that the tacky carpet is a reflection of how he feels about you.

The reason I'm explaining this is because some girls will stop dating a guy because he didn't take her to a fancy enough venue. Too bad for her. You mustn't do this. You never know, for your second date he may book a table at an exclusive restaurant and give you the seat with the riverside view. If a guy takes you to the mall, you go. I admit going to the mall for a date sucks; I didn't like it either but I went. It's only a coffee date. Remember this is only at the very beginning; if he continues to make shoddy date plans, by all means stop dating him.

You Will Get Booty Calls

The best way to avoid booty calls is to get a dating phone which is switched off at an appropriate time each night. I used to turn my phone off at 10 pm and sometimes earlier, mainly because I'm early to bed. By earlier I mean 9 pm not 5 pm. You might be a night owl. Either way, to avoid booty calls switch your phone off after a certain time. By a certain time, I'm talking whatever is reasonable for you. Don't overdo it! Don't switch your phone off at 5 pm if you're expecting a call.

Another way to avoid booty calls is simply don't pick up. *Voil*à, problem solved; aren't we smart?

Men Will Make Sexual Remarks on Dates

I didn't get this much on dates. The whole time I dated I got propositioned once. A guy said something like 'would you consider something short term?' I can't remember his exact words but basically he wanted some 'fun' or rompy-pompy. I responded with, 'I'm flattered but you have the wrong girl.' Thankfully I'd only ordered a small hot chocolate which I quickly consumed before ending the date and heading home.

It's normal to get the odd pervert and I'm using the word 'pervert' lightly. If you keep getting on-going sexual remarks, take a look at how you're physically presenting yourself to men. One client complained that her dates only seemed interested in sex. After working together, I discovered she was turning up to dates wearing a see-through negligee top with her bra visible underneath. In her online dating pictures, she was wearing a very low, black, skimpy top. The first thing you noticed was her impressive bosoms. When I changed her pictures she started attracting a different calibre of male. If this happens to you, try not to dress overtly sexual on dates; the idea is to dress classy and not trashy. If you feel men should take you or leave you regardless of how you dress, that's entirely up to you; I'm merely pointing out that if you're getting a lot of sexual remarks on dates - it could have something to do with you.

Men Will Say They'll Call and Won't.

This will happen! They will also shower you with compliments, they will say things like:

'You're so beautiful; I've never met anyone like you, and it would be great to see you again.'

And guess what?

You'll never hear from them ever again.

What happened?

Nothing.

In simple terms, for whatever reason he's not that into you. It could be anything: maybe it was something you said or maybe he didn't like your voice. There is a myriad of reasons.

If he doesn't make contact after the date, he is not that into you.

You'll Get a Ton of Very Short Emails

You will get so many short or one word emails. Again, I've covered this in depth in my first book *Why Men Ask Dumb Dating Questions*.

Receiving very short or one word emails is fairly standard. Here are a few examples:

'hey'

'Hi how r u?'

'hey beautiful'

'fancy a hook up?'

'what r u up to?'

For all very short emails via an online dating site - ignore, delete and don't worry about it. Men who are interested take the time when writing to you. A man will fuss and stress over what to write to his dream girl. If you're his dream girl, he will take his time crafting the note. He may ask a friend to check it over before pressing the send button and then he'll wonder whether you received the note. Men actually do this. How do I know? I've watched them.

One word messages on dating apps are however completely normal. If you're using a dating app or communicating over a chat or instant-messenger functionality, the vast majority of messages will begin with a 'hi' or a 'hello' and you can respond to these with a clear conscience.

Men Who Send Pokes and Likes Are Not That Into You

This is called window shopping. And you know what happens when you window shop, you look then you walk away without buying. It's the same principle. These men are not into you.

What to do? Ignore of course. I don't think I ever checked or paid any attention to pokes, likes or waves. Neither should you.

Not All Men Will Like Your Look

Have you ever heard the saying:

'You can be the juiciest peach on the planet but you have to accept some people don't like peaches.' Please try and remember this on dates. From a biological perspective all men have a look and a type of woman that they prefer.

Maybe he likes blondes and you're a brunette; maybe he likes athletic and you're slender or vice versa. The good news is that there's a lid for every pot and we're all compatible with more than one person. We're actually compatible with approximately two thousand people each. That's more men than you can date in a lifetime. If he doesn't call you back, there will be plenty of others who will.

Men Will Send You Aggressive Emails

You may receive messages like this

'What's with the two-word emails?? If you really want to get to know me, then give me a call. Sending a two-word message every few days is not a way to communicate effectively in my opinion. I don't play games. I treat people with respect and I don't waste their time or play with them. I expect the same respect back. I have no time for nonsense.'

If you get aggressive emails like the above, or if he sends inappropriate pictures, delete and block the sender. Don't bother reasoning, arguing or defending your corner, block and move on quick. The best response to a fool is silence.

Men Will Talk About Themselves on Dates

This is very normal. I need you to understand this. Many clients complain that he 'only talked about himself'. This doesn't mean he isn't interested in you. He's talking heaps and not asking many questions about you because, in effect, he's showing you what he's got, he's laying his stall out so to speak. He's saying 'this is me, this is what I have to offer and I hope you like it.'

But shouldn't he get to know me?

He will and all in good time. In the meantime, this is an excellent opportunity for you to listen and take notes. Lots and lots of notes!

Men Only Ask for a Date Because of Your Profession

It's true and I think it's called 'networking.' It's a little unfair but that's urban dating for you. Sometimes a man is more interested in your career or profession; in some cases, he's only asked for a date because he's after some free advice.

It happened to me and it may happen to you. A couple of times men only asked for a date because of my advertising background. One guy actually turned up to the date with his company promotional flyer. He asked if I could take a look at his brochure and give some advice.

It's annoying. All you can do is thank him (through gritted teeth) for the drink and end the date. You will feel a little used but *c'est la vie*!

Men Will Ask You to Go Dutch

If this happens to you, please pay your share and end the date first. Don't get offended. Try not to take it personally. From his point of view, for whatever unfathomable reason, he's not that into you; he's not planning on seeing you again so why should he pay for you? Any man who asks to go Dutch is not into you, if your date asks to go Dutch, please don't do any of the following:

- Pretend you left your purse at home

- Tell him you have no cash

- Walk off with paying your share

- Make a fuss or get into an argument.

Simply pay your share with a huge smile on your face and don't see him again. That's all you have to do.

Some Men May Be Married

Unfortunately, there will be the odd male who turns out to be married. Annoying! I once went to a singles event and sat next to a woman who happened to be married. She confessed she was married, going through a rough patch and out for some fun. At least she was honest. The point is, OK it will happen and women are just as guilty as men. If you find out he's married, don't complain and don't explain, simply stop dating him.

Common Excuses to Avoid Dating

Coaching my clients, I am conscious that some of you actually avoid dating, probably because the process isn't always enjoyable. Try not to procrastinate and don't be put off. It's similar to finding an excuse not to exercise: sometimes it's hard to get off the couch but you're usually glad you did. The gratification comes after the event; dating works in the same way.

Meeting Mr Right takes time. It took me approximately two years of active dating before I met my husband; I don't know how long it will take you. I once spoke to a girl who was searching for twelve years. She was incredibly picky. I'm not saying it will take you this long but it *will* take time. It's not a case of attending one event or joining one site and voila. And don't let the excuses take over; you can date and work through your excuses at the same time.

The sooner you start the better. Start before you're ready. You may not be 100% happy with you right now but my advice is start and perfect 'you' along the way.

Back to the excuses. I hear lots of them let's run through some of the more common ones now:

1. Too Busy to Date

No you're not!

I hear this excuse all the time and please don't get mad but I don't believe anyone is too busy to date.

Normally when clients use this excuse and I ask what's keeping them so busy, the first culprit is work, as you'd expect, and second is 'the gym!' Often she won't date because it interrupts her weekly exercise routine.

If this is you start by carving out time in your busy diary. Maybe hit the gym in the morning; that way your evenings are free to date.

It's highly unlikely you'll have dates every day of the week and not every week is the same.

Look at your diary and by all means make social plans. I always tell my clients to make flexible plans, plans that they can change should a date get confirmed.

This is what I mean by flexible plans:

Let's say you're single and dating. It's Sunday afternoon and you're sat at home chilling. You already have dinner plans for Thursday; you agreed a dinner with the girls. On Sunday you get a call from a guy whom you met at a singles party. He asks your availability for a date on Thursday. Oh shoot! Sure, you could tell him:

'Thursday doesn't work and Friday works better.'

You can do this but Friday may not work for him and then you start playing 'date-day ping pong', which can get frustrating and annoying and before you know it you can't meet for another two weeks.

To avoid this back-and-forth, if your date asks and gives three days' notice, there are a couple of ways to manage this either:

- Reschedule dinner with the girls and go on the date. Your true friends will understand, mine always did, they care about you and want the best for you.

- Agree a quick drink date at 6.30pm, and arrange to meet your friends at 8.30pm. Prioritise dating and make social plans that you can work around.

There will be some plans that you can't work around, for example your Dad's surprise 70th birthday party or a friend's wedding. Even then, if your friend's wedding is in the afternoon you could possibly fit in a quick coffee date in the morning. I know we're pushing it but might be possible.

Provided your date is giving three days' notice, you go! And please don't cancel on your date because you'd rather go home and take a bath. Most of the work is turning up so make sure you do turn up. You can take a bath the next day when you're dateless.

The only time you should cancel or reschedule a date is if you're sick or if the sky falls down.

2. Work

Work as I mentioned briefly is a huge culprit. Work will always be well - work. Your employer is never going to say 'sure, you have a date, leave early today'.

If you have a busy stressful job or heavy workload, you have to try and juggle. On days when I had a date after a busy day at work, I would be careful not to arrange any late conference calls or client meetings. In short, try to go easy on yourself as much as possible without getting sacked. It's not forever and as mentioned it's unlikely you'll have dates every night of the week anyway.

One year I hosted a singles party. A couple of girls booked tickets but didn't turn up on the night because of work. It was a shame. They didn't know who they might have met. Prioritise dating over work -without getting the sack of course.

In any case, happy people are more productive, everyone knows that, so it's good for your employer. In exchange for leaving work on time, you get to date, which in turn increases your happiness, which makes you more productive in the workplace. Okay, I'm clutching at straws but you get the point.

3. Too Choosy

Yes, please be choosy, why wouldn't you be? You're a great catch and deserve a great guy. There's nothing wrong with being choosy but don't obsessively nit-pick. By all means, if he's abusive or harms you in any way, stop dating him but, on the flip side, I strongly urge you to open up your 'deal breakers' a little.

Now is a great time to sit down and re-evaluate what is absolutely mandatory versus what is simply nice to have.

Some areas may be non-negotiable: for example, you're a dog lover and it's absolutely vital that he loves dogs too. In that case I understand you can't flex. Maybe check out dating sites geared towards animal lovers. In short go to where the single dog lovers are. In the same vein, if you're a fitness fanatic, join a sports club with a skew towards a male membership.

On the other hand, if you're a wine drinker and he doesn't care much for alcohol, don't ditch him because he doesn't enjoy wine with his cheese; he can always order a soft drink while you enjoy your favourite tipple.

4. Life Event

Sometimes a life event can halt your dating and love life. If you're recovering from an illness, of course you can't date. If you're in therapy for a deep-seated childhood trauma, please don't date; take self-care and get all the help you need. Otherwise date. A life event has to be something serious if it's going to impede your dating. Don't use the fact you got a parking ticket as an excuse to cancel your date and please don't use work as an excuse. Yesterday one girl told me she couldn't date because of a fall out with her friends; she said she was too upset to even consider dating. Honestly?!?!

5. Looking After Elderly Parents or Being a Primary Carer

I have clients who are the primary carer for their elderly parents. They want to date but can't because they're dispensing medicines and working around hospital appointments. In this instance, try to get some help. One of my clients is the primary carer for her mum.

She managed to get some help which freed her up to date a little. She couldn't date much but it was a start. If you're a primary carer, keep your dates short if you have to - but date. Your parents want to see you in a happy relationship.

6. Money Worries

Dating can get costly. There are paid subscriptions for dating sites and apps and tickets for singles events and parties aren't cheap either. Then there's the cost of 'beauty' in the form of regular blow-dries and manicures and so forth. My advice is 'suck it up'. Sorry if that sounds short but at least you don't have to pay for dates. He pays for the dates and he travels to you. Try to see 'the costs' as an investment into your future happiness.

Even if you're absolutely on a tight budget, you can still date. Join free dating sites and apps; they're not the best but something is always better than nothing. Sit in coffee shops and buy water or the cheapest thing on the menu; hang out in museums and galleries, exercise outdoors, all of these are free. Sitting in the park dressed up won't cost you anything either; you never know who might be playing Frisbee or walking their dog.

7. Weight Worries

If you're trying to lose weight you can diet and still date. By all means work on your weight but don't use it as an excuse to stay single. Worst case scenario: wear black, order water and date.

8. I Can't Meet Anyone I Like

If this resonates with you, keep going until you meet someone you do like. I'm going to try and forewarn you a little, in the hope that you'll heed my advice. I've spoken to single girls who have spent most of their prime years rejecting men. No one was ever good enough. Now they're years older, still single, in other cases childless and really regret rejecting men who actually were good enough.

If you're searching for a while and can't meet anyone you like, revisit your deal breakers. Some of the things you think are really important may not matter in the long term. Height was a big deal breaker for me. I'm 5ft 8 and height was important although I was willing to compromise on other things like age and location and I also didn't care about his marital status. Some girls won't date divorced men or men with children. I feel it's a mistake.

Let's assume you've been doing everything right, and you're still not attracting the right men - if this is seriously your problem, and I mean seriously, in this instance it's a question of persistence; you have to *keep going*. It's a little like having all the right qualifications yet not being able to land a job; you keep the faith and keep going. I don't know how long it will take you to find Mr Right but I do know: you gotta be in it to win it.

9. I Hate Dating

If you hate dating, you will stay single. This is like saying 'I hate interviewing'. It would be hard to get a job without interviewing, unless you decide to work for yourself. In the same way, if you hate dating, either stay single or get on with it. I realise this is matter-of-fact but please - get out of your own way. The more dates you have, the easier it becomes. Again sorry if that's not what you wanted to hear. If you really hate dating and have zero confidence maybe try hypnotherapy. What harm can it do?

10. Sporadic Dating

If you're attending events once in a while, maybe checking online dating and mobile apps every now and again this won't work. This on/off approach won't get the results you want. It has to be consistent. You have to commit and do the work each and every week.

Use All the Channels and Resources Available

You can meet men anywhere. Of course you won't want to date all the men you meet - just as well because I'm exhausted just thinking about it. My clients have met their husbands on the tube, in pubs, in the park while walking their dogs, via mutual friends, via twitter, via dating apps, via online dating to name a few. I don't know how and where you'll meet your guy. I do know you have more chance if you go to where the men are.

Here are some popular ways to meet men:

1. Online dating - I'm a huge advocate of online dating. Join as many sites as possible. The subscription costs add up and it can get costly but we've agreed to see these costs as an investment haven't we? The investment is your 'happily ever after'. Make savings elsewhere, for example maybe pack your own lunch for a few weeks or skip the daily, large caramel latte. All these savings add up.

2. Mobile dating apps - love them or loathe them, they're here to stay. You may as well grit your teeth and embrace dating apps because there sure are plenty of men using dating apps.

3. Speed-dating events - search for events in your area. If there are no events in your area, search for events in the next town or city. Sign up and go.

4. Singles parties - again search for events, sign up and go.

5. Networking - ask within your family and friends' networks and circles. Let everyone know you're looking to meet Mr Right. Don't worry what they think: who cares what they think. Remember, it's simply a means to an end. If your friends and family set you up on dates, even if you don't like the date, dress up and go.

6. Work - lots of people meet their significant others in the workplace. Start dressing better for work. Keep it professional and see if anyone is trying to fake meetings in an attempt to get your attention.

7. Your local place of worship will sometimes have matrimonial services. Ask around and sign up.

8. Join clubs/meet up groups, basically anything that interests you where there is likely to be a high proportion of males. Don't join an all-female gym. Apply a little strategy and common sense.

9. Bars, clubs and restaurants aren't always the best places to meet single men. Never say never but if your 'meeting-men plan' consists solely of going out to bars and restaurants, make sure you supplement these venues with other ways to meet men. The downside of bars and restaurants is that you don't know who's single. If all you can manage is one bar once a week, that's slightly better than staying at home.

10. Airports are supposed to be great hunting grounds. If you're off on holiday, get to the airport early and hang around. If you live near an airport and are dateless, it can't hurt to dress up and hang out in one of the airport bars or coffee shops.

I'm going to share with you what I did to meet Mr Right together with the associated results. This is what I did and how I got on.

- Online dating: I was active on nine dating sites yet subscribed to about fifteen if not more. Every time I joined a speed-dating or singles events, the host company would add my details onto their dating site. On one site alone I received over 9,000 views and a total of 1,500 emails. All of which I answered. Some sites produced great results while others not so much. If one site wasn't producing leads it didn't matter as the other eight made up for the shortfall.

- Speed dating and singles event: I don't know how many I attended. It was lots. All my efforts resulted in two leads which didn't go anywhere. I recall attending singles wine tasting, singles dating in the dark, singles balls, singles lock and key parties, a singles cinema club - to name a few.

- Gym: I joined a mixed gym and no one significant asked for my number.

- Family and friends: I put the word out to my family and friends. Most responded with something like 'oh I don't know anyone'. My entire network generated one lead - via my aunty in California who called her sister-in-law in London who called me with a lead. That's all I got, one lead. I'm hoping you'll do better.

- Matrimonial list at the local temple: I joined the matrimonial list at my local temple and paid £35 for an annual membership. The matrimonial list was simply a list of your vital stats i.e. age, height, education, profession. No photos. This list generated one lead. A mum called on behalf of her son and asked to speak to my parents. Nice mum but it didn't work for me since I didn't live with my parents.

- Matrimonial agency: The only reason I joined is because my Dad asked me to and he offered to pay. I signed up mainly to stop him from worrying. I didn't have much luck in the form of quality leads.

- Coffee shops/galleries/museums/festivals/meet-ups: I did all of these and, from memory, can't remember any leads.

- Running club: I joined a local running club which boasts 2.5 k members and I attended their summer and Christmas parties. No one asked for my number. I would also run along the river with my make-up on; no one ever stopped me - with one exception.

I remember one Saturday while dating my husband. We were in the early stages of dating. I woke early and went for a run, taking my usual route. I was looking forward to our date later that day and feeling happy. I ran up the road when a guy tried to get my attention. I continued running around the corner and *two* men who were standing next to each other did the same. They started waving and again tried to get my attention. I remember thinking 'now that's odd.' The reason this stands out in my memory is because it was the first time something like that happened. When I sit and think about it, I can only conclude that I must have been emanating positive pheromones that day; in other words, I was happy.

My advice to you is to get happy or at least fake it a little. And how can you get happy when dating is getting you down? Find your passion and start doing all the things you love. I don't know which channels will work for you, try everything and adjust accordingly.

I have spoken to girls who refuse to actively date, because they want love to 'happen naturally'. She feels if they meet 'naturally' it's a sign that he is the one.

They're hoping to find Mr Right while out and about their daily business. Maybe they'll lock eyes over the water cooler or maybe they'll be flung together during a wind storm.

Let's say you're flung together by the wind during a storm. I mean it's natural right? During this storm you get blown about a little; you cling to the nearest lamp post, to find a guy clinging to the same lamp post. He risks his life by going after your woolly hat which the wind knocked off your head. You take these signs - wind + him risking his life to get your hat + you're both in the same place at the same time and conclude your prayers have been answered. After all, God works in mysterious ways. It was meant to be, right?

I hope you don't harbour such fantasies. There are no statistics which prove that couples who meet without 'trying' are more likely to succeed then couples who meet less spontaneously. I hope you're savvy; I hope you socialise - I hope you're stacking the odds in your favour by trying as many ways to meet men as possible.

Others won't online date because they fear someone they know might see their online profiles, honestly, who really cares? Last time I checked, taking charge of your love life wasn't a criminal offence. Searching for your soulmate is nothing to be embarrassed about. Once you're happily married, you won't care either.

Some girls won't consider dating apps because they feel they're only for hook-ups. Sure there are good and bad men everywhere. To say that all men on dating sites are liars, freaks, cheats and only after a hook-up is farfetched. In amongst the rubble there are some real gems.

Put yourself out there and try to drop the negativity. I've spoken to girls who think online dating is the worst thing in the world. And something she would never consider. I wish she would because that's where the men are. The only thing wrong with online and dating apps is that you're not doing it. If it makes you feel better, my husband and I met online.

Keep an open mind. Give it a go. You have nothing to lose. Yes, it's arduous and at times soul-destroying but it does work.

Here's a little loving advice to help you on your way:

- Date men you wouldn't normally consider dating.

- Attend events which are out of your comfort zone.

- Give the divorced men and the men with children a chance.

- Say 'yes' to invites even though you'd rather stay at home.

- Go to events alone. Some girls won't attend events because they don't want to go alone, they don't want to be perceived as a loser or a billy-no-mates. Get over it and go. You can't always count on your friends; they may not want to go when you want to go. Maybe they're busy with work – you and I have already covered using work as an excuse.

- Don't judge men so quick. Don't think you know 'What he's like,' based on a few texts and messages. Granted, sometimes you really can tell, especially if he starts sending sexually charged messages. I'm not telling you to settle or accept crumbs; I'm urging you to break down your barriers and keep an open mind.

Duty Dating

If you've never heard the term duty dating, let me introduce you now.

Duty dating is dating men who don't tick all your boxes or who may not tick any at all.

Here are a few reasons to duty date:

- To help define what attributes in a relationship are really important to you.

- To challenge your pre-determined 'deal breakers'.

- To meet as many men as possible before finally going exclusive with one suitor.

- To stop you obsessing over one guy.

- To restore your faith in abundance and there is an abundance of men out there.

- To help finesse your date game.

Isn't it a complete waste of time?

No. You're giving men whom you'd never normally consider, a chance. Who knows, he may be 'The One'. Anyway what harm can it do? You're only meeting for a quick coffee or drink date. Nothing ventured, nothing gained. At the very least you've met another human being. He may even introduce you to some of his single friends; likewise, he may not be for you but he might be suitable for one of your friends.

Still not convinced?

Again, it's like interviewing for a job. You apply for a job; they call for an interview. It's not your dream job but you go anyway. You reason that, at the very least, it's good interview practice. At the interview they may consider you for another role, perhaps a role that offers more career prospects.

Duty dating works in the same way.

Set up dates with men who don't tick all your boxes. If he asks keep an open mind and go. All you're doing is meeting for a coffee or a quick drink; it's not like you're about to say 'I do'.

Isn't it unfair to the guy?

No! This lucky guy gets to spend time with gorgeous, hot you who looks and smells amazing; he should pay you for the privilege. You're probably the best date he's ever had. And if you're easy to be with and show gratitude, you will do more for his ego than a hundred therapy sessions. He will walk out feeling likes he's conquered Mount Everest.

If you don't feel comfortable or feel you're leading him on, remember - it's only a date. Nowhere does it say 'thou shalt be 100% interested in the other person before thou even thinketh of accepting a drink date'.

Sure sometimes you can learn about a guy from his messages, but there's no way you can really know until you've met them face to face. So go anyway! You never know. It's all good dating practice especially if you're new to dating.

Have I done enough to convince you?

I hope so because I'm off for a coffee break.

Multiple Dating

Multiple dating or circular dating as it's sometimes referred to is a must. Let's use a quick analogy. Multiple dating is like trying on different pairs of shoes before finding the perfect pair.

Shoes come in all shapes, sizes, colours and types: open, closed, flip-flops, sandals, high heels, court, long boots, ankle boots, espadrilles, the list goes on and on. A little like men. I'm not saying men are shoes. I'm saying: when looking for a new pair of shoes you try on various pairs before finding the perfect pair. In the same way, by accepting a date all you're doing is 'trying out' a man to see if he might be a fit. That's the whole *purpose* of dating. To see whether there may be a fit. The more men you date, the more chances you have of finding the perfect guy.

Don't shy away from multiple dating. Let's run through why you should multiple date.

- You get to date 'widely' before finally deciding on 'The One'.

- You date from a place of abundance rather than from a place of lack or fear. You know if he didn't call, he wasn't that into you. No need to fret or worry because clearly there is someone better intended for you.

- It's healthy and positive and allows you to confidently and fearlessly 'next' all men whom you're not completely sure about.

- It stops you obsessing over one man. You should never obsess over one man. As one falls, another takes his place.

My most favourite is: when you're out on a date and before the date has even ended, other suitors are already texting or trying to call you. Ah abundance.

Is it manipulative?

No, it's smart! In the beginning, it's silly to put all your eggs in one basket. And it's not like I'm saying you should *sleep* with multiple men; that's not what I'm saying at all. Again, let's run through the job-search process. You don't stop your job hunting because of one good interview; sometimes interviews can take three or even four rounds and come with a written assessment. The job is not yours until you have a signed contract. In the same way, until you're exclusive, you're free to date whomever you please.

If you didn't already know, men will multiple date until he finds the one and you should too.

Survival of the Fittest

When it comes to finding a long-term mate, I hope you know by now that there has to be a fair transaction. This transaction in the beginning is usually 'looks v resources'.

This doesn't mean all men are shallow and all women are gold diggers, not by any means. Men are attracted to looks because they're visual; Mother Nature wired him that way. He wants a girl who looks after herself because he's thinking 'gene carrier.' In the same way women are attracted to resources. Again she's wired that way. She wants to ensure he can look after her and her offspring.

It's all about survival and continuing the human species. The reason we fall in love, pair off and produce offspring is because if we didn't as a species *Homo sapiens* would die.

Love and romance is Mother Nature's way of ensuring our survival as a species.

Dating can be viewed as survival of the fittest, mainly because it's hard work. The fittest will survive.

Some people get so fed up, frustrated and jaded that they decide to give up. Months or years later some regret their decision while others make peace with it. The good news is that it's never too late to date. Even if you once decided to give up, you can start again.

Don't give up at the first hurdle either. And there will be many hurdles, correction - *many, many* hurdles: to recap men you like won't like you and vice versa; men will try your patience; men will arrive late for dates; many will arrive without date plans; they may not look like their profile pictures; you will get stood up at least once or twice. Get prepared for your fair share of timewasters too.

There will also be the odd guy who turns out to be married or who is only looking for short-term fun.

Don't hold any illusions. When I was dating one of my friends was actually envious. She thought I was getting wined and dined and 'having fun'. Did I have fun? I wouldn't exactly describe my dating expeditions as 'fun'; they were a lot of work. Some dates were better than others and many times staying single seemed like an attractive option; at least I wouldn't have to endure any more bad dates. I always bore in mind that giving up guarantees one outcome only – staying single.

In order to 'survive' get smart. Don't take advice from single friends who aren't dating; they don't know what it's like. Stay away from man-haters too. Get support from girls who have what you want or single girls who are also searching for love. Surround yourself with positive, supportive people and ditch the naysayers. It's tough out there. If anyone makes you feel bad for working so hard in looking for love, ditch them.

Only give up if you don't mind staying single. If you genuinely don't mind, by all means stop dating. Don't use 'giving up' as a trick mechanism: don't think that, if you stop trying, maybe the Universe will get tricked and throw you Mr Right.

Sorry - not likely and slight fantasy.

All right, never say never but give yourself a helping hand. If you're serious about Mr Right, giving up is not an option.

You may of course meet Mr Right without trying. There are plenty of stories about meeting Mr Right while on a random night out, this may happen for you, In the meantime keep going and stay in the game.

PART THREE

GETTING OUT THERE AND MEETING MEN

Online Dating

Men are everywhere although, granted, sometimes it may feel like there's a man famine. We've already touched on online dating a little. Let's go into more detail.

I'm a huge advocate of online dating. As you know by now, I joined multiple dating sites and the majority of my clients are on ten plus dating sites. If you're only subscribed to one or two sites, join more. Yes, it can get costly but we've already covered that and agreed to 'suck it up'.

If you're not online dating at all, please sign up today. Every single girl who is serious about looking for love should be online dating and using dating apps as a basic minimum. Your opinion of them and whether you like online dating, is irrelevant. It's where the men are and you gotta be in it to win it.

Not all dating sites are the same; some are better than others. Generally speaking, paid dating sites are better than free dating sites, probably because there's some investment on his part. Every site will have its share of time wasters, the odd married guy who is looking for a little action. I didn't say it was going to be fun. I'm not promising fun; dating is work. You will have your fair share of highs and lows, many one-word emails, men who post younger-looking pictures, men who stand you up, plus the odd crazy.

If it makes you feel better, I didn't enjoy dating much. As I said my friends thought I was having lots of fun but that couldn't have been further from the truth. Dating was simply a means to an end. The good news is that it does end - and I really enjoyed dating my husband, I would look forward to our dates and we had lots of fun. Other than that it was mainly a case of 'grin and bear it'.

Here's how to online date effectively:

To forewarn you, the first few days and weeks generate the most amount of messages from prospective suitors, don't get over-excited in the beginning and assume the activity levels will remain constant. They don't. Initially you're the new girl in town, new girls join all the time and you will soon become stale. After a few weeks your online activity will start to dwindle.

This is standard and to be expected. Don't worry; there are steps we can take to increase your activity levels. Every dating site is different but here are a few things common to all that usually work:

- Update something in your profile. Even if you simply add a full stop or change one word within the profile section, that's enough on some sites to move you to the top.

- Change your username - another trick to avoid staleness.

- Update and rotate your pictures will keep you fresh and new.

- If the website or app has a 'premier listing' or 'spotlight' functionality, get involved - especially if it means more men are likely to see you.

Keeping it fresh is so important. If you're bored of your pictures, chances are he will be too. Don't worry, new men join every day. While you may be 'old' for the stalwarts, you're 'new' for the newbies since they haven't tired of seeing your profile yet.

Try not to get complacent, if your pictures aren't working (you'll know because no one is writing to you) change or rotate them. The number of times you update your pictures is limitless. Update each month if you have to.

The Written Profile

Most dating sites have a section that allows you to write more about yourself. If you're stuck with what to write, you're not alone. Let's cover this now:

Firstly, don't go overboard when completing this section, don't waste time thinking of clever things to say and don't worry about whether you're coming across as funny or popular.

The written profile only needs to be one paragraph in length or two short paragraphs maximum. There's no need to write a long essay. He really isn't interested in your life story, not at this stage. Men don't read the written profile anyway. Yes, he will have a quick skim to check you're not a stalker, needy or clingy or trouble. Of course, if he gets any hint that you might be trouble, high maintenance, too hard to please, needy or clingy he won't bother - neither would you.

Your written profile shouldn't say anything about anything. You don't need to say very much and the less you say the better. Keep the profile light and fun. Whatever you do, don't write anything negative for example don't say:

'I'm feisty and competitive, looking for someone who can keep me challenged.'

Anything like this will turn him off in a big way. Turning men off is not the result we're looking for. Rightly and wrongly, men will interpret 'feisty and competitive' to mean you're stubborn and argumentative. In case you didn't know it, men want an easy life. They don't like drama. All they want is to come home and relax. They don't want to date or come home to someone who is always challenging them. If you need to be challenged, join a local debating society or take up a hobby that feeds this need.

Here are other things not to say in your profile:

'Time wasters need not apply'.

Most men don't consider themselves as time wasters; men don't think 'today I'm going to waste someone's time'. Plus, even if you say 'time wasters need not apply' you will still get your fair share of timewasters; it comes with the territory. Also, writing 'time wasters need not apply' implies that you're jaded and fed up - and that all you attract are time wasters. Even if that's true, it's not in your interests to create a negative impression.

'Only looking for men who are serious about a relationship and marriage'.

Writing anything like this will make men run the other way and they will run fast. Any sniff or even the tiniest whiff that you want marriage is enough to turn him off. Sorry but that's how men think. In the beginning you can't mention marriage, children, a long-term relationship or anything that alludes to anything other than 'simply getting to know each other'.

The List

Don't write a list of what you like and don't like. For example, don't write:

'I like chocolate truffles, Louboutin's, pink champagne, long Sunday-morning leisurely walks, lazy weekends reading the papers, fresh coffee, French pastries, cut flowers, sunshine, dogs, beaches, travelling to unknown places with only a map and a blanket, spontaneity'.

Anything like the above unfortunately comes across as 'high maintenance'. It's akin to giving him an upfront list of what he has to do to keep you happy. He may not like coffee or he may enjoy doing sport at the weekend. Play it safe and don't create lists.

In short don't write anything derogatory or negative because that's a major turn off and keep it short and simple. At this stage he's more interested in what you look like and your pictures.

Usernames

Your username should represent something physical about you because men are so visual. Ellen Fein and Sherrie Schneider bestselling authors of *The Rulesbook* (I'm a huge fan and also a *Rules* certified coach) recommend using a celebrity reference for example:

Cameron Diaz lookalike

This makes complete sense since nearly every man on the planet knows what Cameron Diaz looks like, or they can at least search for her online. The reason for using a celebrity reference is because every man has a look or a type. He either likes tall, petite, curvaceous, athletic, blonde, brunette, fair skinned, olive skin - we could go on and on.

He likes what he likes and there's absolutely nothing you can do about it, other than to accept it. Sure you could change your hair colour but if he likes short and you're tall, there's not much you can do. This is actually great news because if he doesn't like your look he simply won't contact you. Less time wasted for everyone.

The majority of my clients aren't comfortable using a celebrity reference as a username and admittedly I wasn't either. If you're not comfortable, select something which reflects you physically for example:

Brown-eyed girl

Slim brunette

Green-eyed girl

Avoid using obscure, arcane usernames. Even if they mean something to you, they won't mean anything to him. Use everyday words which are easily understood. Remember it has to prick his attention. If it doesn't resonate he will skip over your profile. Here's what I mean by obscure usernames:

Bright2sky

Happyhazzers

sweetmoonpie
Tromso
begonyabcn
Notimenospace
Tootefruit
Daglo
Sd8me

In the above real life examples, these usernames mean nothing to anyone else other than you and you're not dating you. Also don't create a negative username either. The aim isn't to create a negative first impression.

In advertising copy, the experts recommend using normal, everyday words instead of long words. Why? Most people don't understand long words. Long, complicated words turn customers off. Yes, the advertiser is very clever but using words which are only understandable by a few won't help sales. Apply the same logic when it comes to dating.

If you will only date men who understand a username such as those listed above for example, that's fine as long as you understand you're targeting a very small handful of men. If they do understand your clever wordship, they may not like your look which means even less dates for you. It's in your interests to keep it simple and cast a wide net.

Pictures

Your pictures are key. The pictures really are that important. I have helped many clients with their profile pictures. I'm sharing some notes to help you on your way.

- Don't post any old pictures. You want the best pictures possible.

- Don't wear overly sexual or revealing clothing.

- Don't wear oversized clothes or anything baggy. Wear clothes that flatter your figure.

- Have a plain background; don't post shots of you standing in your bedroom with your breakfast bowl balanced on your unmade bed.

- No pets nor animals of any description, no holding babies nor children. Posting a picture holding a baby doesn't show off your maternal side. It scares men off.

- Don't post ten pictures; you only need two or three maximum.

- Don't post selfies.

- No photos which have been stretched or are blurry.

- No pictures with a cap/hat.

- No holiday snaps.

- No pictures with a mask or anything that hides your face.

- No pictures of you with food/after a meal/before a meal. No food period.

- Don't post pictures where you've cut off the other person.

- No pictures of you in big groups or with friends on a night out.

- No pictures in bikinis.

- No drunk pictures or holding a wine/champagne/beer glass.

- No pictures of you running, cycling, skiing, snowboarding, hiking, snorkelling, parachuting, on a boat, on holiday.

- No selfies taken in the car.

- No pictures of you with a female friend - how's he supposed to know which one is you?

- No pictures of you with a male friend – a no-no for obvious reasons.

Sometimes clients will tell me they've been online dating, really trying and not having any luck. I look at their profile pictures to find that they aren't even posted straight – or worse. Sometimes she's posing standing next to a giant snowman wearing a woolly hat, or she's underwater diving. All great but how can he tell what you look like when your hair is covered with a hat or you're underwater in a wet suit and a snorkel?

The 'pictures' for some of my clients are a real journey. I'm going to share the average journey hoping you'll avoid these mistakes.

It starts with the girl posting any decent picture which she deems OK. She thinks it'll do. She doesn't love it but she doesn't hate it either. She'll post online regardless and then wonder why no one is making contact. Some girls will purposely post 'any old picture' online. She reasons 'well if he sees me at my worst and he's interested that's a good sign.'

I understand this point of view although I never shared it. Men are visual. If he doesn't like what he sees he won't make contact. And why would you want to show your worst side first? It's a little like having a CV which is full of typos and badly formatted or going for an interview and talking about how you were fired for sleeping on the job; no employer will take the risk. It doesn't matter how much they like you personally; they have a business to run. In the same way Mr Right wants someone whom he can be proud off, someone who adds to his life not deducts from it.

After starting with whatever pictures they can find and after some persuasion the girl may ask a friend to take some pictures that are better but not great. So I'm begging, pleading, with you to post the best pictures possible. You want to look the hottest possible. My strongest advice is to book a photoshoot. This is the single, smartest decision you can take to invest in your love life. If you want a better man, post better pictures. Your pictures are like your CV. People spend lots of time crafting the perfect CV because it's so important as a first impression; approach your pictures with the same mind-set.

Here are some additional notes and some reminders to help you:

- We need two really good pictures as follows, a very good head shot and full body shot.

- Pictures should be recent and real. All pictures should be taken within the last six months. Posting pictures which are a true representation and likeness means less worrying later.

- No black-and-white or sepia shots, no 'arty' shots either.

- No pictures in traditional dress unless you still live in your native country.

- You need four to five decent pictures in total. That number allows you to rotate your pictures every couple of months. Keep it fresh.

Now is not the time to be shy. Unless you live in a conservative culture or you're trying to attract a conservative guy, please don't wear loose clothing. If you have to cover up for cultural reasons, try and wear fitted or skinny jeans and long-sleeved fitted tops.

If your culture is less conservative, it's all about fitted dresses, skirts, jackets and tops in bright colours that flatter your figure. If you're not happy with your weight, wear black and inject some colour through make-up or jewellery.

If you hate having your pictures taken as I do; get over it and book a shoot anyway. Take a friend if you have to but go. If you'd rather die before posting professional shots online – make sure to post some anyway and preferably before you die!

For anyone who claims they're not photogenic. Neither am I. Thank goodness for Photoshop. Every little helps and it's a jungle out there; get all the help you need. We don't want fake overly Photoshopped shots but a little nip tuck here and there and maybe erasing the odd breakout is all good. Long live Photoshop and good lighting.

Preparing for the Photoshoot

The photoshoot needs some preparation. Here are a few tips to ease your journey.

1. Ideally find a photographer who includes hair and make-up as part of the price. Otherwise you will have to organise your own hair and make-up. Hair and make-up included makes life much easier.

2. There are photographers who cater purely for the dating market. They take pictures for dating profiles only. Some are better than others. Shop around and ask to see their portfolios. If you know any local matchmakers, it's worth giving them a call to see who they work with or recommend. Most matchmakers work with photographers; again, do

your homework and check any recommendations are unbiased and void of any kickbacks.

3. Once you've found a photographer, tell him or her exactly what you need the photos for. Tell them specifically 'I need a good headshot and a good body shot for dating'. We don't want any glamour-type shots; that's not the result we're after. Tell them you want the pictures to look 'natural'. Don't worry, they won't judge you; chances are they're probably dating too. Don't be shy with what you want. A clear brief enables the photographer to work out how best to serve you. Make sure they're fully briefed. Work with them; they want happy customers.

4. Next, organise your entire outfits, including jewellery, any accessories and shoes. Ordinarily you'll need about two or three outfits. The cost or chosen package usually determines the number of outfit changes. Check what is and isn't included as part of the price.

5. The head and body shot need to be different. We don't want the same look in both pictures. Typically take one outfit for a day look, one for a lunch-with-the-girls look and one for an evening look. Take your time selecting the outfits. Book a personal shopper if you need too. Most department stores offer free personal shoppers, check them out. If your hair needs cutting or colouring, get this organised ahead of time. Ensure your eyebrows are perfectly maned; consider either lash extensions or false lashes - and don't forget your nails.

6. On the day, pack your chosen outfits plus one or two extra; it won't hurt. At least it's packed in case of any last minute mind-changes. Allow anything from half a day to a whole day for the photoshoot, taking into account any travel time. In short prepare and plan for the photoshoot. Take your time but don't take forever. Don't take months,

we're talking a couple of weeks. If you need to travel a little further to get to the photographer, travel.

7. Ideally we want the shoot to produce about four to five decent pictures. I only managed two great pictures which I used to rotate but hopefully you'll do better. Four or five decent shots in your dating war chest allows ample stock for rotation purposes.

8. Upload your new pictures onto all your social media sites. You never know who is looking at your profiles or Facebook. Who knows, they may be a friend of a friend who really likes your look.

9. If you post new pictures and you still don't see a great uplift in numbers of contacts, get in touch or ask a trusted friend who will tell you the truth. If the pictures aren't working, have some more taken. Don't skimp on them, other than diet and exercise they are the single most important investment you will make. When I swapped my 'taken at home' pictures for professional shots the number of men who started writing increased tenfold. Your pictures may end up getting circulated further than you think. For example, my husband, unbeknown to me, downloaded my dating pictures and saved them on his phone. Later I found out he'd showed these pictures to his family, friends and work colleagues.

10. Finally, photoshoots can be tiring. Make sure you eat or take some energy bars and water or fruit with you. You normally get your pictures back a few days later. It all depends on the photographer and what you paid for.

11. When you get your pictures back, look through them or ask a trusted friend to help pick two to post online. Some photographers include Photoshopping within the price. Check to see what the package includes. Work with the photographers to Photoshop them but don't go Photoshop crazy; the pictures have to look like you.

Overanalysing his Profile and Messages

Now we've covered off your pictures and profiles, let's move onto his online profile. A common mistake made by women is overanalysing.

Don't overanalyse his written profile and don't analyse every single word he writes. Read his profile but don't go looking for or inventing trouble where none exists. You really can't tell much from a few pictures and a written profile.

Here's what I mean. There are girls who won't date a guy because he wrote:

'I would love to meet you.'

Don't zone in on the word 'love' and conclude any man who uses 'love' in the first message must be emotionally insecure and needy and therefore you can't date him. And don't reason that the word 'love' should never be used lightly. The fact that he has so haphazardly said 'love' when you haven't met must mean he doesn't fully comprehend the deeper meaning of the word 'love' so again you can't and won't date him.

Another example. If he writes:

'I love eating chicken and enjoy swimming' even if you're a vegetarian who can't swim give him a chance. He's not about to make you eat chicken burgers and enter you for a swimathon. Don't judge him because your preferences don't perfectly match.

Let common sense prevail. If his profile says 'I'm currently serving two years in prison' or 'I was once arrested for tax fraud' - give him a miss.

Don't pore over words and overanalyse. If he signs his text with an X in the form of a kiss, this doesn't mean he wants sex, must be a sex addict and will mistreat you.

Lots of men sign their texts with an X and guess what? It doesn't mean a thing. In the early stages of dating, please don't overanalyse. Ignore a man's words and focus on his actions.

Specific actions we're interested in are:

- Is he trying to date you? By this I mean, is he trying to set up dates? Is he asking to meet for a coffee or some other activity where he gets to see you?

- Does he pay for dates?

- Is he happy and willing to travel to you?

- Does he consistently ask for dates each week?

- Does he ask for Saturday-night dates?

Men who write and write but never ask for dates are called pen pals and we don't want pen pals. Some men will happily converse with you online and never ask for a single date. These men will waste your time provided you let them.

The trick here is to stop communicating if he doesn't start asking for a number or a date. I remember having a conversation with a distraught client. She had spent six months writing to a guy who never asked for a date. Later she found out he was talking to multiple other women and as you can imagine got upset. The fact that he never asked for a date nor even bought her a drink was very telling. If he's not trying to date you, he's not into you; it's as simple as that. Men who are interested want to see you and hear your voice. These are the types of men who deserve your attention and time.

Here are another couple of examples of over-analysing a man's profile –

- In his profile picture he wore a cap – she concludes any men who wears caps in their profile pictures are buyer-bewares.

- He wrote that he enjoyed occasional fast food – she concludes any guy who eats fast food isn't grown up, her reason being that only children eat fast food and therefore she can't date him.

The same applies for his dating pictures. In the beginning try not to play detective for example if he hasn't uploaded pictures onto the dating site, don't assume this means he must be married, cheating or a buyer-beware. Don't judge or jump to conclusions too soon. My husband never uploaded any pictures; he preferred to email them. After he wrote he emailed his pictures separately. Some men like to keep their business private. Sure you will get the odd man who is married - I'm pretty sure you'll find some married women online dating too. As long as he sends you pictures privately and he's trying to date you, it's all good.

If he has uploaded pictures and you don't like them, or you find him average and are not sure if you like him, give him a chance anyway. You never know, once you meet him in real life, he may blow you away.

The same again applies to Facebook and social-media sites. If he doesn't have a Facebook account this doesn't mean he's hiding something. I personally know many men who never use Facebook. My elder brother doesn't have a Facebook account and some of my husband's friends who are single and searching also don't use Facebook. They have absolutely nothing to hide; they simply don't use Facebook and don't understand what the fuss is about. Come to think of it, I know many decent, hardworking, honest men who never use Facebook. Just because they don't have a Facebook account this doesn't make them criminals, liars or cheaters. Even if you feel not having a Facebook account is outdated, focus on what matters - which are his actions.

I would urge you to look at the bigger picture. Don't focus on every single word and hack it to death. Remember, different words have different meanings for different people. Don't waste time obsessing or overanalysing before he's even had the chance to take you on a date.

Online Messages:
Which to Ignore and Which Deserve a Chance

One thing you will discover when online dating is that not all messages are the same. Let's run though this now. Online dating emails fall into four categories

These categories are as follows:

1) One-word or short emails

As already mentioned you will get lots of one-word or short emails, for example:

'Hi'

'Hey'

'You look nice'

'Wanna hook up?'

'Hey gorgeous'

Men who write and continue to write one-word emails can be safely deleted. There's no need to reply to any of these messages. You will get a ton of one-word emails; it's typical and very much part of the process.

2) Generic cut-and-paste emails or form letters

These are messages that say nothing about your profile in particular.

Here's an example:

'Hey you have a great smile and may I say you look stunning in your profile. Anyways here's a little about me. I live and work in London; I work as a marketing manager and really enjoy what I do. I believe life is too short to waste and you have to seize the day. I enjoy the outdoors and I'm a keen cyclist, I also enjoy traveling and I've travelled extensively throughout US and Europe. Well that's a little about me, if there's anything else you'd like to know do get on touch.

Paul

Paul.h@gmail.com

08756 142 654

These types of messages are called 'form letters' or 'cut and paste' emails. He hasn't mentioned anything in your profile specifically, he's only written about himself. I can guarantee he has written the same generic messages to zillions of girls.

These types of messages are also a delete. There's no need to respond.

Don't worry, most men who are interested will write again. A man doesn't stop chasing because you didn't respond to one message. That said - don't *test* men; don't wait until he's double messaged as a way to test his interest.

3) Cut-and-paste email but semi-personalised

These are messages similar to type two but semi-personalised. He may mention your username or write something about your profile. However, the bulk of the message is a cut-and-paste.

These types of messages are generic messages although top-and-tailed for you, the recipient. They're easy to spot and here's an example to demonstrate:

'Hey blue eyes

I'm always stuck when it comes to this type of thing and I hope your job as a teacher isn't too stressful. I've found it's always good to give a little about me, this way you can see if you like what you read and we can take it from there.

Here's a little about me, I work as a lawyer; my job is both demanding and challenging although I enjoy what I do. The hours are long and in my downtime I like to relax by watching movies, hanging out with friends. I live by the mantra 'work hard, play hard' I think it's important to have balance in life. I'm also into martial arts and I'm hoping one day to explore this further. I am highly ambitious and driven. I guess there are lots I want to achieve. Anyway that's a little about me...

Hope to hear from you soon,

Jack.'

These types of emails are a little deceptive to the novice datee because you think he's written about your profile. He's mentioned you're a teacher which could imply that he's taken the time to read your profile.

The way to respond to these types of messages is to write:

'Hey, thanks for the note.'

That's all you need to write. After responding, wait to see what he comes back with. As a general rule, if he doesn't ask for your number or for a date within seven exchanges - forget about him.

The seven exchanges are four messages from him and three from you. If after seven exchanges approx. he continues to write but isn't in any rush to date you, move on. He is a time waster.

4) Men who take the time to read and write something about your profile

These are the types of emails we want and with some practice you'll be able to spot the differences between the different email types.

A personalised email means he has taken the time to read and writes something about your profile. Here's a sample:

'Hey blue eyes

I see you're from London. I used to live in London too but now I reside in the Midlands. Are you born and bred from London? Do you really rollerblade too? Great picture by the way. The blue suits you. Would be great to meet for a drink providing you're free?

Mick'

There are only ever four categories of messages. The more you date the better you become at working out who stays and who gets deleted.

Let me talk you through how I structured and approached online dating.

I would log on three days a week. My designated online dating days each week were Tuesday, Thursday and Sunday. Each week on these days I would log on to check messages.

The first thing I would do was to delete all messages which were either:

- One worded or short

- Generic cut-and-paste

- Any other inappropriate type of message for example sexual types or simply moronic. These were deleted within a nanosecond. Press the delete button and off they go, never to reach your inbox again.

Next I would delete any guy who lived outside the UK. I wasn't interested in dating anyone who lived on the other side of the world. Too much hassle. There were plenty of men in the UK. Plus, long-distance relationships are hard and honestly I simply didn't want the hassle; I focussed my search purely on the UK.

After this I would see what was left and I would respond accordingly.

The deleting and cleaning up my inbox could take five, ten or twenty minutes depending on the number of emails received that week, bearing in mind that each week brought different results.

You're welcome to apply the same logic.

Approximately 99% of the messages received via dating sites and apps will probably wind you up the wrong way provided you let them. Don't get yourself into a tizz and don't get mad if you receive yet another stupid message, otherwise you'll spend a whole lotta time getting mad - and this is not good for your blood pressure.

Delete any messages which are one-worded or inappropriate. Don't spend any time focusing on these types of messages. It's a complete waste of your time and headspace. Do the cull as quickly as you can. Focus only on the good messages. Focussing your attention on the time wasters gets you nowhere. Spend as little time as possible talking, thinking or complaining about these types of men. Clouding your mind with the time wasters, means less mind space to recognise a gem.

Mobile Dating Apps

Mobile dating apps are increasingly popular and here to stay. Some are free while others are paid; some have a bad reputation and are criticised for being all about 'hook ups'. The truth is you have to go to where the men are and there are plenty of men on mobile dating apps.

To quickly address the 'hook up' criticism: Friday and Saturday nights in bars and clubs supply ample opportunities for men and women across the globe to hook up - but this doesn't mean you should stop frequenting bars and clubs. Anyone looking for a 'hook up' can hook up anywhere including at work. Regardless of what you think about mobile dating apps, every single girl who is serious about meeting Mr Right must sign up.

Here's how to navigate

Dating apps are like instant messaging or chat. Dating apps are more casual in nature simply because the nature of chat is casual.

Check dating apps the same day you check your online dating messages, that is: Tuesdays, Thursdays and Sundays. That way you're not constantly online and visible, plus you get a well-deserved break. This method of spacing things also allows you to space out your interactions.

Chatting can be time-consuming. As a general rule, give each guy ten to fifteen minutes of chat per session and see how the conversation progresses. Ten to fifteen minutes is a general, ball-park figure. Often you will have multiple chat conversations with multiple men happening at the same time. Be prepared for this and make time to log on and manage as best you can. You're only chatting three days a week and those days are already marked in your dating schedule. Log on, chat with whoever initiates contact, give each guy ten to fifteen minutes per session and promptly log off.

How to progress the conversation

The whole idea of dating apps is to meet men and get dates. If he didn't progress to a date during the first session, give him another chance provided he is still initiating the chat.

If he asks to progress the conversation to another chat app, for example WhatsApp which seems to be the most popular option or asks for a contact number, supply contact details for whichever you're most comfortable with. If you're not comfortable talking on the phone –try and get comfortable, otherwise you'll have to endure the headache of trying to organise a date via text or chat.

If he continues to chat via another chat application, once again, give him another ten minutes and see how the conversation progresses. If all he ever writes is:

'How's your day?'

'Are you at work?'

'Are you busy?'

You can simply ignore.

If you don't want to continue the conversation onto another app, simply tell him:

'I don't use WhatsApp!'

I actually deleted WhatsApp from my phone because I found it too intrusive. It didn't matter: men texted or called instead. As human beings we're wired to find 'the path of least resistance'. If it's easier for him to chat on Whatsapp, he will; if he can't get you on Whatsapp, he'll text or call.

The majority of interactions via dating apps and chat will start with the ubiquitous 'hi' or a 'hello'. This is very normal; you respond back with 'hi'.

Some online dating sites also have an app functionality. In this case treat it in the same way. For example, if you log on via the dating site, treat each message like you would for online dating which we've already covered. That means ignoring all one-word emails and only responding to messages where he's taken the time to read your profile.

If you sign up via a dating-site app, treat each message like you would chat, which means you reply to all one-word messages and give each guy ten minutes of chat per session.

If you're a fan of *The Rules*, Ellen Fein and Sherrie Schneider say you can either give him ten minutes as explained above or you can give him four exchanges to ask you out. Both methods work, it's up to you which one you prefer. If you're new to *The Rules* get in touch and I'll point you in the right direction.

Are dating apps inferior to other ways of meeting men?

Some girls won't digital date whether that's online dating or dating apps because they feel meeting face-to-face is better than meeting via a screen. I hope you don't think like this. Digital dating is simply another way to meet men and it's here to say. I would encourage you to embrace it. The trick is to supplement digital dating with other ways to meet men.

Should you un-match?

No! You're way too busy to spend time 'un-matching' men. There's no need to confirm your disinterest. If he's un-matched you, don't worry about it. It's great feedback since it means he's not into you. One less lead to worry about. When I was dating, I remember one dating site gave the option to 'cancel interest'. Men would 'cancel' me and I'd think "doesn't he have anything better to do?" - like talking to others girls for instance? I never cancelled or unmatched anyone; I couldn't be bothered.

Do dating apps work?

Yes! At the time of writing I have multiple clients who met their personal Mr Right via mobile-dating apps. You may hate them and think they're all a waste of time but, regardless, sign up anyway.

Speed Dating

Speed dating is another way to meet men. I never had much luck with speed dating despite attending my fair share; hopefully you will do better.

All the many events I attended resulted into two actual dates. That was all - two! One date turned out to be too short for my taste which was disappointing. It was hard to tell at the event since we were seated. If you're attending speed dating events lower your expectations.

Speed-dating events are different to singles parties in so much as women stay put while the men move around. Speed-dating events generally all follow the same format which runs something like this:

On arrival most participants normally congregate at the bar. There is usually a bar. The events I attended were generally hosted in nice bars or clubs. If your local place of worship is hosting, then there may or may not be a bar.

The hosts will greet you and hand you some paperwork which usually includes a name badge and a 'match' sheet. The 'match' sheet may be called something different; it doesn't matter because its function is the same. In essence it's a small pro-forma used for the purpose of recording his details and whether you feel he is 'match' or not.

Next you're assigned a table number, let's say table three. That is your speed dating station where you remain for the event duration.

Each session per guy lasts about three to four minutes. If the tables are positioned too close to each other, you'll hear his conversation with the girl sitting at table two. Try to tune out.

At half time there's usually a short interval; this is your best opportunity to let as many men as possible see you. If you need to use the bathroom, walk there slowly, do what you have to do quickly and walk back to your table again as slowly as possible. Otherwise stand at the bar and order a drink or stand somewhere so men can see you. Why? At speed dating you're usually sat down, it's hard to judge each other's height, or top-to-bottom appearance. The interval is prime time to show off your hot dating outfit and matching shoes; we can't let all that effort go to waste now can we?

After the event has ended, don't hang around. Hand in any paperwork and leave. Some people stay at the bar to talk. Not you. Get your coat and leave.

The hosts collect everyone's match sheet. They'll use these sheets to work out who matched with who. This means looking at who ticked you and vice versa. You'll get the results either by logging onto the host's website or they may forward them via email.

All matches are notified of each other's email addresses or contact numbers. The hosts don't normally share any personal details other than your email and/or contact number but check with the organisers when making the booking.

Speed dating events typically last about 1.5 hours depending on the number of attendees. Again check with the event organiser, and if you attend a lot of speed dating events, ask the organisers for a discount, maybe they can offer you a discount since you're a loyal customer. Don't ask don't get - so ask. They can only say no.

A top speed-dating tip, which took me a while to figure out, is to tick everyone. You may not feel comfortable doing this, regardless, tick everyone. I was having such poor results at these events, sometimes I matched with one or, if I was lucky, two men. I decided to 'rig' the system and started ticking everyone.

Why? Well, because you're only notified if there's a match. If he ticked you but you didn't tick him back, they won't notify you. Even if you match and he makes contact and, you decide he's not for you - simply ignore his email or call. Or maybe go on the date anyway; it's all good practice.

How to dress

Don't wear work dress. If you're attending after work, change before you go. Change in the work bathroom. If you're not comfortable with your colleagues seeing you all dressed up on a random Tuesday evening, find a department store with bathrooms. Worse case, find a coffee shop with toilets, buy water and use their bathroom to get changed; it won't be great but who cares. If you know you have a date or an event, plan ahead and ensure your day wear is easily glam-able.

You can't go wrong with clothes in nice colours that flatter your figure. Don't dress frumpy and don't wear clothes that cover you from head to toe unless your culture dictates this. Men are visual; they have to 'see' you first. Do your nails and wear your hair open. Don't tie your hair in a ponytail unless it's a classy ponytail. Wear big, round earrings and take extra care with your make-up - and wear heels.

Bottom line is: make an effort, don't turn up scruffy. Dress like you're going to a party. Glam it up and think feminine. It's better to overdress than underdress and now is not the time to dress understated. If you feel overdressed simply pretend you have a ticket for the hottest after-party in town. Pretend you're the special guest at Leonardo Di Caprio's new film premier.

When to turn up

Don't turn up late; turn up ten minutes early if you can. Greet the hosts, collect the necessary paperwork, either use the bathrooms to freshen up or head to the bar and order a drink. Don't stare at any men; pretend they don't exist. (Okay, you can, provided it's with the corner of your eye, just don't let them catch you staring at them.) Everyone will be busy checking everyone else out so act nonchalant, happy, calm and positive.

What to expect

Take your seat and wait for the event to begin. As stated the men move around for the three-to-four minute slots. The hosts usually ring a bell to signify when time is up and it's time for them to move on. When it comes to the 'conversation' follow the man's lead and let him ask the questions. Your responses should be light, fun and playful. Remember, you're amazing; nothing fazes you. Men will probably ask the same types of questions; they usually do. All the answers are in my first book titled *Why Men Ask Dumb Dating Questions*. Smile your way through it. If there's a pause or a silence, simply smile and silently count to yourself. It's not up to you to fill in the gaps.

Go solo or in a big group

Absolutely go solo or with one friend only. The friend can be male or female; it doesn't matter as long as you're not part of a big group.

If you and your friend are both speed dating, don't make a point of pointing her out to men. If he asks 'did you come with anyone?' Don't say 'yes I came with my friend who is over there'. This makes men uncomfortable. They're conscious you'll swap notes and he'll start watching what he says. The idea isn't to make him feel uncomfortable; it's not a test he has to pass.

Never ever go in big group. This is not an occasion to hang with the girls. A night out with the girls can be arranged any time. This is 'work.' I recall at one speed-dating event and a girl sitting at the next table who came with five of her friends. She wasn't shy in pointing them out either. She found it all hilarious and seemed to relish the men's discomfort. I watched as men squirmed; for them it was awful. And awful for him means no dates for you.

Some events allow you to take a friend for moral support. I did this once but wished I'd gone solo. Friends are great but they keep watching and making notes and it was a little off-putting although you might be okay with it. My advice is go solo or with one friend only. If you're going solo and need moral support call a friend before and after the event. I did this once and it did help. Another option is to arrange to meet your friends somewhere after the event. The more events you attend the easier they become. Dress up and go.

Bumping into old dates

If you're activity dating, at some point this will happen to you. It happened to me twice although neither were old dates as such. They were men whom I'd conversed with via a dating site or we'd had a coffee date. If you recognise him and now he's sat opposite you, greet him normally and let him do the talking. If you've exchanged emails online and he recognises you from your online profile, act like you don't remember. Don't fill in the gaps or try to remind him. Admittedly it's very uncomfortable and a little embarrassing but stay cool; it's only four minutes. Consider it character building.

Managing nerves

Now is not the time to get nervous. We don't have time for nerves. All right of course you'll get nervous. In the beginning I would get nervous too, especially if going solo but after the first few events solo I stopped getting nervous; it stopped bothering me.

If you're nervous try reframing the events in your mind. Tell yourself 'it's just a meeting'. Pretend you're simply heading into town to meet some people about some work stuff. And repeat 'all good things are happening to me under grace in perfect ways'.

Does it work?

Yes, it does. It never worked for me but I have clients who met their husbands at speed dating events.

Should I be having fun?

Having 'fun' is a bonus. If you're not having fun or enjoying speed dating, don't worry I never enjoyed it either. I would always have very stern words with myself and force myself to go. The last thing I wanted to do on a cold, dark, wet Saturday evening was to dress up, walk to the tube station, attend a speed-dating event, which was always on the other side of London where invariably the men were never my type anyway. That wasn't my idea of fun. If you're having these feelings, I hear you. Regardless of how you feel, you still have to go.

Last Saturday night, my husband and I were walking back from dinner. It was cold, dark and wet and my mind flashed back to a couple of years earlier: I was in my room talking myself into attending a singles event. Then the flash-back was over and I was walking back from dinner hand-in-hand with my husband with the leaves blowing around us - to say I was overcome with a huge moment of gratitude would be an understatement. You *must* dress up and go.

Singles Events

Singles parties are different from speed dating events. This type of event is normally hosted in a bar or a club and the numbers are bigger. Depending on the event, some attract up to two hundred singles. They usually start with some type of ice breaker - lock and key is hugely popular. There's also some form of entertainment whether it's a live band or a tribute act.

Some singles parties kick off with a round of speed dating. Check with the hosts to find out what's included. If speed dating is offered, sign up because it's a great opportunity to meet men in a shorter time frame. Don't worry if you turn up and don't like anyone. Some men arrive fashionably late so stay until the end because you never know who may walk through the door. You of course must arrive early. Often singles parties have an after party, there's no need to attend the after party; once the main event is finished, head home.

How to dress

Dress to stand out. The majority of girls will wear black; maybe, try red, cream, white or gold. Dress glam. I'm not talking ball gowns but dress like you're heading for dinner at a Michelin-star restaurant. Wear something distinctive, for example a hat, or a piece of jewellery, maybe a statement necklace, anything that helps you stand out in a good way. I once hosted a singles party in London. Nearly every man who called after the event and asked about a particular girl mentioned something visual. One said 'the girl in the red dress'. Another said 'the girl in the stripy top'. If he didn't get a chance to talk to you at the event, let's say there were too many men fighting for your attention. In this instance sometimes he'll call the event organisers to ask about you. Help them remember you.

When to turn up

Turn up on time. Don't be fashionably late. The main events don't last long so make the most of the event.

What to expect

Lots of people standing around awkwardly staring at each other while wishing they were someplace else instead. Sorry sometimes it's like this.

Normally the host will greet you. If speed dating is offered, sign up because spaces tend to go fast and make sure you arrive early enough to take advantage. Otherwise, grab a drink, get involved in any of the ice breakers and wait for men to come to you.

You can't talk to any men first but you can walk the room. Keep moving and don't stand still. Head to the bar to get a drink. By all means use the bathroom to re-apply make-up then come back in and keep walking. If a guy takes the time to talk to you, talk to him and don't be rude to anyone. Men talk to each other.

Give each guy ten to fifteen minutes, after that make an excuse; say something like 'well, it's been great talking to you' and walk away. You only have two hours. Two hours broken down into ten-to-fifteen-minute segments best case (minus when you're not speed dating, at the bar or hiding in the bathroom) equates to approx eight men being able to approach and talk to you. If it's a large event, you don't have time to waste.

Don't spend all night talking to the same guy; allow as many men as possible to talk to you. That said, don't worry that you're skating over opportunities; if a man is really interested and he didn't get a chance to talk to you at the event, he can always follow up with the event organisers the next day. Remember to help him out by wearing something he and the organisers can remember for example 'the stunning girl in the gold sequinned dress.' Chances are you're the only girl wearing a gold dress because most girls turn up in black.

Go solo, not in a big group

The same rule applies as for speed dating: either go solo or with one other friend. Never ever attend in a large group and don't spend all evening glued to the same spot or seat. I once saw a group of five girls all sat down at a table, they walked around a little (together) and then they all sat down. I don't think any men approached them. It's too intimidating for a man to approach such a large group. I bet they went home and said the event was rubbish.

It's easier if you're solo or with one friend. Some men come solo too although they generally hunt in packs of two. Sometimes friends can be a hindrance - she may decide to talk to men on your behalf. Big no-no! Men have to talk to you first. Either that or she may feel uncomfortable and you end up babysitting her. Pick your sparring partner carefully. My advice is - go solo.

Bumping into old dates

Again, it's much like speed dating. If you're actively dating, it's very likely that you will bump into old dates. If you've spotted each other, don't worry he's probably cringing too, especially if you had a bad date or some history. In that case he will try his best to avoid you.

Here's what to do: pretend you haven't seen him even though you have. Walk right past him as if you've barely noticed. He's there for the same reasons as you and he doesn't want an old date ruining his chances of meeting 'the one'. If he does approach you, greet him cordially like you would an old acquaintance, say something like 'oh hey how are you?' Make small talk and after a couple of minutes say 'well, it's great seeing you, I'll be right back'.

Walk off and that's the end of that.

Managing nerves

Again, the best way to manage nerves is to reframe the event as a networking evening, pretend you're heading to a networking evening or you're auditioning for the latest block buster. Dress and act accordingly. You may have to act a little but it gets easier the more you do it.

Growing stale

Sometimes attending the same events too often means growing stale. Men may stop approaching since you're 'old news'. To stop this happening, mix up your events. Don't attend the same events week in, week out. Attend events hosted by other companies and look up events held in different towns and cities. Don't become the dress in the window that won't sell. If there are absolutely no events in your area or in the neighbouring areas, consider hosting your own.

Does it work?

Yes, although I don't know how many events you will have to attend before he finds you. There's no way of predicting it: you might get lucky and meet him at the very first singles party or you might have to attend lots and lots. Your job is to plant a big smile on your face, dress like a celebrity, turn up, and see who talks to you.

Networking – Family and Friends

Your network of family and friends is another avenue to meet men. If you trust their judgement, ask them to help. Meeting men through family and friends offers some security - at least he comes pre-screened.

Let's assume you trust your family and friends. Contact everyone within your network who you feel could help. You could take them out for dinner or a drink or you can simply call them. Explain that you're looking to meet Mr Right and, if they know anyone, could they be sure to call you? If friends and family take time and effort to organise dates on your behalf, show some willing and go. It's only a quick drink date most probably.

There's no harm in exploring this route especially if you're single for a while. In short, do a little 'find a date' campaign. Call everyone who you think can assist and ask if they know any eligible bachelors.

Most will nearly always say 'no I don't know anyone' but don't let this defeat you. I heard this plenty too. Simply tell them 'Ok great however, if you think of anyone let me know and here's my contact number'.

Quick word of caution: enlist your family and friends carefully. Don't ask anyone who doesn't have your best interests at heart - and don't ask anyone who is known to gossip.

If family and friends do help, apply some sensitivity when answering any questions. If they ask 'how did it go with the guy I set you up with?' handle your response with some care. Don't say 'omg he's not my type, how could you?' It's better to say something non-offensive such as 'thanks for thinking of me, he sounds interesting, I guess we'll see what happens'.

They obviously set you up with him because, on some level, they felt it could be a match. Let's give them a point for trying. If after a few months of searching you're still single, have another ring around. Keep yourself front of people's minds, no harm reminding family and friends what a great catch you're for one of their friends.

Another avenue is to try and attend as many family functions as you can. I didn't do this very well although I tried. It became tiresome having to explain why I'm still single to all those nosey aunts. Again, hopefully you'll do better.

Other Ways to Meet Men

Let's cover even more ways to meet men. Some we've discussed although no harm in running through again.

Work

According to some stats, many people meet their significant others at work. Makes sense given how much time the majority of people spend in their workplace. Start dressing better for work and, as always, apply some common sense. Keep it discreet and don't become the target for office gossip. Even if there are no decent men at work, it's still good to dress better for work - I have a client who met her husband on the tube during her work commute.

Places of Worship

Some places of worship host singles events and hold matrimonial lists. You know what to do: sign up and dress accordingly.

Matchmakers

Ideally find matchmakers who match-make exclusively for men and allow women to join their databases for free. Join up it doesn't cost you anything. Most matchmakers who charge both sexes won't admit this but they generally have a large female base. They either have to recruit men on your behalf or they offer men free or discounted membership to join their books. Whatever methods they employ; it doesn't matter as long as they find you a match. No harm in working this to your advantage: find the matchmakers who charge the men and let the women join for free.

Meet-Up Groups

Join as many as you want. There are meet-up groups especially for singles, join what you like and turn up. If there are no suitable meet-ups in your local area, search within the next area or consider organising your own.

Bars and Restaurants,

Generally speaking, bars and restaurants aren't a great way to meet eligible bachelors mainly because like I said you don't know who is single. My single girlfriends and I tried the bars and restaurants route too. At that time we were four single girls. Provided we were dateless, our plan included heading out weekly, usually on a Friday or Saturday evening. We decided to get smart and target places with a higher proportion of men. After some research we found places in London that were popular with the types of men we wanted to meet. Sometimes only two of us would go out; it all depended on who had dates or not. We would dress up and head to a different place each time. None of us did very well. Men would talk to us but, from memory, our regular expeditions didn't result in many dates. For the most part we had a good time however. Sometimes we'd dance and other times we'd meet for dinner.

I'm not saying don't head out to bars and restaurants; something is always better than nothing. Sitting in a sports bar beats sitting at home solo on a Saturday night.

Private Members Club

Pricey but worth a try, or if you have a friend who has membership see if he/she will let you tag along.

Any Type of Sporting Club

Literally, anything at all based on your interests. Again, apply some strategy; don't join an all-female club or group. Apart from that, join almost anything for example a running club, badminton club, squash, tennis, rollerblading or golf club etc.

Professional Balls, for Example Lawyer's Balls.

If you have professional friends, tag along to their parties and events.

Charity Events.

If you're interested in a particular charity, get involved.

Political party events.

If you support a particular political party. Join their societies, groups or clubs. You never know who might be sitting next to you.

If you live in a small town and there are absolutely no prospects of meeting suitable bachelors, get online or consider moving to a larger town. Also, before I forget now is not the time to plan any extended holidays or long trips. Every single girl I've spoken to who took an extended trip always came back single. I'm not talking about living and working abroad; I'm talking about girls who want to meet Mr Right and take anything from three months to a year off to travel.

I once spoke to a woman, she was forty-two, single and really wanted to meet Mr Right and start a family. What do you think she did? She took a three-month trip around Italy. She figured she might meet a nice Italian while out there. Unfortunately, she didn't, she came back single and three months older.

Let's say you're waiting to hear back about your dream job: would you organise an extended trip? I don't think you would; you'd wait to hear about the job first. I'm not telling you to put your passion for travelling on hold. I'm asking you to think smart. If you really want to go travelling. Go but either book a shorter trip or, if you do plan an extended trip, at least find singles events in the host country and sign up. Even better find holidays or trips geared specifically for singles.

Dating Review

Now that we've covered all the ways to meet men you will find that once you've started dating, it's important to stay fresh and current. You can't grow stale.

Every three months, set aside some time and evaluate what's working and what isn't. During my advertising career, after each campaign we would all get together for a 'wash up' meeting. The sole objective of this meeting was 'campaign evaluation'. We would look at what worked and what didn't, including the results. Amongst other metrics, we would measure how many people responded to the campaign; how many actually bought the product or service; how many enquired but didn't buy; where they saw the campaign; which communication channels produced the largest number of sales plus a few others metrics.

What's all this got to do with you? We're going to apply the same thinking. Every few months, look at what's working and what isn't. Ditch whatever didn't work and do more of what works. What works for you won't necessarily work for someone else.

Here Are a Few Things to Consider.

- Which dating methods are working for you?

- Which are a waste of time?

- Are your pictures appropriate for digital dating? If you're online dating or using apps, rotate your pictures and see how this affects things. If one picture works well, make this your primary picture.

- If your pictures are getting dated, update them. I had to literally force one client to update her pictures. Her rationale being men had already seen her old pictures and they might wonder why she posted new pictures. Silly! He won't remember, especially if your pictures are poor or outdated. There are so many girls online. Thankfully she did update her pictures and was surprised when men who previously looked at her profile but never wrote were now writing to her. They didn't even remember her earlier pictures. Amazing what new pictures can do. It's not that men are dumb. It's more that your previous pictures didn't leave a lasting impression and now they do.

- Are you making the most from social media sites? Have you uploaded the best pictures possible and refrained from sharing your life story online?

- Have you checked out the competition with a small 'c.' Log onto your dating sites and apps and, if possible, do a search. A thirty-two-year-old female searching for a thirty-two to thirty-five-year-old male is competing with girls aged anywhere between twenty-three and thirty-five. Have a peek at how you 'look' online compared to the other profiles.

- Ask yourself is there anything more you can do that you haven't already done? The answer to this is always 'yes;' there's always something more you can do, even if that 'more' is buying a new lipstick or updating your wardrobe. OK this may not get you Mr Right but at least you'll feel better.

It's All About the Eyeballs

I'm going to draw another quick reference from advertising. A key step to any successful advertising campaign is targeting the right type of customer. The more customers who 'see' or as we say in advertising the more 'eyeballs' on our campaign the more chances to sell.

Unless customers see the ad, there's little chance of brand engagement let alone them actually buying the product or service. In the same way unless he sees you first either online or in real life he can't engage.

Get out there and remember: we want eyeballs. Eyeballs or visibility help you stack the odds in your favour. Bear in mind many men will fall at the first hurdle; they won't even make it to the date stage. If your 'lead' generation is low or depleted, it's time to find more leads and that basically means finding more ways to meet men.

As covered earlier, every week will bring different results and no week is the same. For example, one week you may have a great week - let's say you attended two events and three men asked for your number then, at a networking event, a cute guy also asked you out. That equates to four possible leads. At this stage each one is only a lead or a prospect. Just because he asked for your number doesn't mean he will call. Even if he does call, you may not want to date him anyway.

At the beginning of one week I once had twelve leads, by the end of the week I was left with one. Either I didn't like them or they didn't call or they didn't follow up, or they called but didn't ask for a date. What to do? Set about joining more sites and attending more singles events.

If all of this sounds like hard work, that's because it is. Finding Mr Right is a serious business.

Action and More Action

Action is your friend and taking action is so important. There's no point in creating a vison board, meditating daily, having faith, if there's no action.

When it comes to dating here's what action looks like:

- Looking after yourself and taking impeccable care of YOU.

- Getting date ready. Make sure you're prepared, ready and organised for dates.

- Booking a professional photoshoot and posting the most flattering pictures online.

- Creating a winning profile.

- Signing up to events and more events.

- Using as many channels as possible to meet men.

- Turning up when you don't feel like it.

- Staying positive.

- Keep going when things are slow.

- Moving on quickly from bad dates.

It has to be continual, consistent, persistent action. Some girls will date for a period of time, a month or a couple of months, then get fed up and stop. I call this yo-yo dating. Sometimes she'll even delete all her profiles. Or maybe she'll attend one singles event, feel so traumatised by the experience and vow never to go again. That's it; nothing will make her sign up to another event. If this is you, don't yo-yo date. You gotta be in it to win it, otherwise be prepared to stay single.

Don't worry, it's not forever and it does eventually stop. And I can tell you, all your bad dates, no shows, men who looked nothing like their profile pictures fade away as a long distance memory.

Taking action really helped me through. If I turned up to an event and there was no one I liked, I'd try not to despair. I'd think 'well never mind, there's another event next week let's see what that brings'.

Make sure your diary is constantly full of things you're doing or planning to do to meet men. It will keep you going.

PART FOUR

HELPING YOURSELF

Opening Up Your Deal Breakers

A great way to help yourself is to relook at, and potentially open up some deal breakers. I'm not suggesting you accept anyone. This isn't about settling for the worst. May the best man win, someone whom you will love and who really loves you. This man is going to be your husband, best friend, maybe father to your children, son-in-law, brother-in-law, uncle and confidant, he will care for you when sick, celebrate your successes, slay dragons on your behalf. Phew tough brief. You want to pick the 'right' guy.

I hope you don't have impossible deal breakers. Here's what I mean by tough deal breakers.

Only willing to date younger men

You're in your early to mid-forties never married and want to start a family. You will only date younger men. Never say never and some men do like older women. You might hit pot luck. Unless he's looking for an older woman. It would be smart to open your age deal breakers and include men at both ends of the age spectrum.

Searching for lifestyle

You're in debt but searching for a lavish lifestyle. You're hoping to meet a rich man who can give you the lifestyle you crave. Not likely. If you can't manage your own money, he's unlikely to trust you with his finances. If you're only dating him for a certain lifestyle what happens if he becomes bankrupt? The only person who can give you the lifestyle you want is you.

Height

You're short but will only date taller men. Generally taller men are looking for tall girls. If you're a short girl who will only date men who are 6ft or taller. Maybe open up your deal breakers to include men who are 5ft 10. A couple of inches may make all the difference to meeting Mr Right.

Unwilling to relocate

If you're not willing to relocate that's completely your choice. In that case, focus your search on local dating sites and events. No one said you have to pack up, leave all your friends and family and move to the sticks or the other side of the world in order to find love. If you're searching for a while, having no luck in your area, maybe try looking in the next town or city.

Unwilling to date men with children when you have children

You have children but won't date men with children. You're searching for a single childless man. If you have children, open up your search to include men who also have children. It's tough for a single childless man to take on another man's children. If you really want a single childless man, at least be open to having a child with him. Most men want children.

Dating men with a university degree when you have none

I once spoke to a girl who barely finished high school. Her main criterion in looking for a husband was his degree qualifications. If this is a deal breaker for you, open up your search to include men who are degree qualified and men who aren't. Some of the smartest most successful men on the planet aren't degree qualified. Richard Branson comes to mind.

Men from a different ethnicity or race

Maybe you find men from a different ethnicity or race very attractive. You can't relate to men from your own race. Again if you're searching for a while and can't find what you're looking for, maybe re-consider men from your own race too. More choice for you. Lucky you!

Dietary requirements

If you have special dietary requirements for example you're a strict vegetarian, start by searching for other vegetarians. If you can't find what you're looking for, maybe open up your search to include pescatarians. I was talking to one girl. She was thirty-nine years old, never married and childless. She really wanted to meet Mr Right and settle down. She was searching for a single, never-married man with no children who didn't eat meat, fish or dairy. She wasn't willing to relocate, date divorcees or date carnivores. I say, good luck!

If you're dating for a while without much luck, run through your list. Look to see if your deal breakers are too strict. It could make the difference between being happily married and staying single.

Common Dating Mistakes
Made by Women

In my profession I see many women make mistakes. Mistakes which often hold back their chances of finding love. Here are a few of the common mistakes. Check if you're guilty and if you're guilty, please stop.

Chasing Men

Girls don't chase boys, men know this. He knows it's his job to chase and pursue. Let him come to you. When you chase a man not only does he find this scary, but you're no longer a challenge or a chase. And men love a challenge and a chase. Don't short-change him. Give him the thrill of the chase. As women we already do too much, we raise families, build homes and careers, support our friends and families. You don't need to chase men – one less thing for you to worry about.

Opening Up Too Soon

Women love to talk and often we're guilty of oversharing, It's the way we're wired. At the outset don't open up too soon. Firstly, dating isn't therapy; secondly, he doesn't need to know about your silly ex or how you single-handily put food on the table while raising your only son. Too much too soon. In the beginning the less you say the better. Keep your cards close to your chest. Another reason to zip it is that most dates don't make it past the first date. If you live in a small knit community, you don't want random men knowing your life story. Men talk to men and it's in your interest to protect your reputation.

Not Giving Men a Chance

Give men a chance and don't judge too quickly. Unless he's abhorrent to you, accept the date and go. It's only a date and don't worry about the long term. It's too soon to worry about the long term, anything can happen and circumstances can change. Don't reject him because he lives too far. Don't worry about having to spend hours travelling on the motorway or about the cost of train tickets or travel plans because he comes to you.

Unrealistic Expectations

High or very unrealistic expectations are another mistake. Here's what I mean: expecting a man at the first meeting to totally sync with you, expecting him to know when you're hungry, and expecting him to know what you want to eat at exactly the right time. All these expectations are totally and entirely unrealistic.

Dumping a man because he didn't open the car door or pull out the restaurant chair is downright picky. Men do open doors, they open restaurant doors all the time and they always let you walk in first. Opening car doors or pulling out chairs in restaurants is indicative of zero. These are not signs of a great husband. What's more important: the fact that he opens car doors, or the fact that he books in advance, makes date plans, pays, travels to you and is steady Eddie with weekly dates? Of course as you know, it's the latter.

Unavailable Men

Don't date married men or men who are separated. If you are dating a separated man, at least keep your options open by multi dating. Otherwise only date a separated man if he's actively pursuing a divorce. A few things to consider when dating separated men are that sometimes they go back to their wives, and often there are children and finances to consider. Don't put yourself in a position whereby you've dated him for a few months, and now he's decided, for the sake of his children to give his marriage one more chance. This is the outcome we're trying to avoid – which is *you* left with nothing.

Even if he has nowhere to live, his wife kicked him out and you feel sorry for him, don't take on his problems. You don't know what happened in the marriage. Any man who still lives with his wife (whether they share a bed or not) yet claims they're divorcing should still be considered married.

Play it smart, he can always come find you after his divorce is underway - provided you're still single by then.

Showing Up When You Don't Feel Like It

One of the first rules of success is showing up when you don't feel like it. Who knows what might happen if you show up. He has to see you before he can ask you out. No matter how you feel, show up.

Red Flags Versus Pink Flags

Don't go nuts if he calls at 10.10 pm and you go to bed at 10 pm. He doesn't know your sleep timetable. The best way to manage this is to turn your phone off at 10 pm. He can't call if the phone is off.

Also don't go crazy if he calls you 'princess' or 'darling'. These words don't have sexual connotations. He probably called his last girlfriend princess and maybe she liked it. He thinks you might too. He doesn't know for you these words are offensive. How can he? He's only just met you.

Don't get mad if he doesn't know your dietary requirements straight away. He won't know about your low carbs, no meat, no dairy, no sugar, no alcohol, no-nothing-past-6-pm eating regime. Go easy until he gets to know you better.

Having worked with male clients, many are just as baffled and confused as you are. They don't know what to do for the best. Some girls want to talk on the phone, others don't. They're treading carefully and feeling things out as they go along; they're just as bewildered as you. The vast majority of them don't mean to offend or hurt you.

Playing Detective

In the beginning don't play detective. By detective I mean asking to check his Facebook, arranging to call him at home and only on his landline, arranging a video call in order to 'see' that he lives alone and isn't secretly hiding a wife and ten children in the broom cupboard. There's no need. Watch his actions. Actions will reveal everything you need to know. By actions I mean, he is trying to date you? Travel to you? Does he pay? Is he consistently asking for Saturday dates? It's very easy to tell if a man wants you. If he wants you, nothing stops him from seeing you. If he doesn't want you, nothing will make him stay. He will make you know either way.

Believing All Men Are Cheaters, Liars and Buyer Bewares

You can't expect to attract a great guy with this mind-set.

What to Do When Fed Up and Things Are Slow

Feeling fed up with dating is a normal part of the journey. It comes with the territory. Expect to feel fed up lots. The trick is managing and preparing for these 'low' periods because these cycles are inevitable. I was fed up probably every other week when I was dating.

If you're fed up yet not doing the work - do the work and then we'll talk.

If you're doing the work, the scenario may run something like this. You're out and about, online dating, on dating apps, attending Meet Ups, singles events etc. yet nothing is happening.

By 'nothing is happening' I mean 'where is Mr Right already?' Sure you're getting asked out but none qualify as Mr Right yet. Often it feels like a waste of time, you're adamant it won't happen for you.

What to do?

Keep going and keep trying. Sorry if that's not what you want to hear. Even if you're fed up, you have to stay in the game. And you will 'win it' providing you keep going when things are slow.

Even when 'nothing is happening.' Things are actually happening for example:

- You're getting better at 'dating' and becoming more confident every day.

- You're re-defining your deal breakers and really looking at what is and isn't important.

- You're working out and hopefully looking after yourself, maybe eating better and getting fitter in the process.

- You've probably also made new friends. Whether you join a single support group or attend singles events, I bet your contact list has grown in some way.

- You're also getting smarter. While 'nothing is happening' you've probably read more books, watched more films, maybe even started a new class.

- While 'on a date' you've tried out new restaurants, discovered new places that you didn't even know existed.

In short you're growing, improving and becoming a better person.

Here are things you can do when times are slow

-   Get a makeover

-   Update your dating wardrobe

-   Update your dating pictures

-   Join more dating sites

-   Sign up to more dating apps

-   Sign up to more singles events

-   Have a declutter

Here are ways to help manage those pesky dating blues

-   Exercise

-   Start a healthy eating plan

-   Try out a new recipe

-   Learn a new language

-   Learn to play an instrument

-   Watch movies, read books, go to the theatre, to exhibitions and plays

-   Start a singles support group

-   Take a bath

-   Spend time with friends and family

-   Laugh – watch some comedy

-   Work on your world-domination plans

I'm sure you can think of other ways too. Use this time wisely, once it's gone it's gone. It never comes back. In the meantime, there are an infinite number of things you can do. Go do them.

What to Do If Continually Dateless?

If you're actively treating dating like a full time job yet still dateless, if you're doing the work and not getting any dates, something is wrong. It's time for a little dating review and some honest feedback from a trusted friend or a dating coach. Your family and friends won't always tell you the truth because they don't want to hurt you.

Start by asking yourself a few questions

- Could you dress better?

- Are you presenting yourself in the best way? Are you looking after yourself?

- Are your deal breakers too strict?

- Are you high maintenance?

- Are you a Debbie downer?

- Does what you're searching for exist?

- Would you date you?

- Do you think you're awesome?

- Can you try harder? Could you take more actions to meet men?

Have a little brainstorm; the exam question to answer is:
'What more can I do to attract and meet Mr Right?'
Brainstorm alone or with a trusted friend.
Make a list, turn your list into a plan and go action your plan.
Quick disclaimer, there is always more you can do.

Taking a Break from Dating

If you're contemplating taking a break from dating, the first question to consider is 'if you were looking for work, would you take a break?' Sure you would but it wouldn't be a long extended break. There are bills to pay.

If you want a break from dating, take a small break. I'm talking a couple of weeks absolute maximum. Personally two weeks is too long but I'm trying to keep you happy and reach a compromise.

Don't take a long extended break. It's time you're never going to get back. And none of us are getting any younger.

If you're contemplating taking time off in order to 'work on yourself', for example if you're thinking:

I need a break and a complete dating withdrawal. There's no way I can even think about anything dating-related right now. I need to focus on me. I need to heal and search within'

No problem: 'do the inner work' and simultaneously date. It takes time to meet Mr Right you can perfect as you go.

Don't listen to anyone who tells you to 'take a break' either. They mean well but everyone who gave me this advice is still single.

In short, don't take a long extended break from dating.

If you've totally lost your mojo and really need a break - OK but at least keep your online dating channels open. That way your tentacles are still out there. Deactivating all your online dating accounts and apps, not showing up to singles events, is a great way to stay single. You can take a 'break' once you're happily exclusive, engaged or married. Anyway every single weekend if you're dateless, and there will be a few, you get a mini break. If you have no dates, you can comfortably switch off.

Managing Family, Friends and Loved Ones

Most of the time family and friends are on your side. They want to envelope you with their love. We turn to them because their words are soothing. They make us (mostly) feel better. However, their sugar-coated advice is sometimes harmful because it prevents us from taking the necessary steps to make real improvements. Sometimes it can hurt when yet another man doesn't call back after what you thought was a great date, or when you haven't heard from a man who you thought loved you.

A word of caution: those close to you may not always tell the truth. If you're single for a while, there could be something fundamental holding you back from meeting the one. If you're working hard to meet Mr Right, loved ones want to support you and the last thing they want to do is offend or make you feel worse about your situation.

Managing Critical Family

Some are blessed with wonderful, supportive families, others aren't so lucky. A very common dating problem, and one I also experienced, is dealing with negativity from family.

Often their criticism comes from a place of love. They don't mean it. Really they don't. Hard to comprehend but mostly they are worried about you. They want you happy and, yes, agreed, they have a funny way of showing it.

Here's some advice for managing critical family.

Keep it to yourself. Only share on a need-to-know basis. Don't share more than you need to. If in doubt zip it.

Agree with them. I found this easier than arguing or getting them to see my point of view. They don't appreciate how much 'work' it takes to meet Mr Right. It's exhausting explaining that the dating landscape isn't like it used to be and you're trying.

When I was dating my Dad would call every Saturday for a status update. At first I would tell him who I was dating. He was worried about me and my reason for sharing was mainly to stop him worrying. This approach slightly backfired. Most weeks he'd start the conversation with 'what happened to that guy from last week?'

Well... if you're dating, many men don't call back and many you won't like anyway. If you share too much, after a while your family start thinking there's something wrong with you, they may start thinking it's your fault.

Here are a few things said by loving and caring family members everywhere.

'You've left it too late.'

'There are no good men left.'

'You're too old; your age is working against you.'

'I told you to start looking sooner. Now you're much older and it's harder for you. By the way Jessie the girl you went to school with is married and her son is now eight.'

'I told you to marry Johnny; he was a great catch. You made a mistake; you never listen.'

'You're not getting any younger; you should have started your own family by now.'

If your loving, caring and supportive family members say any of the above. Simply agree.

Just say 'yes yes you're right I left it too late.' Or 'yes there are no good men left.'

After a while I found it was easier not to argue or challenge. Family can't even start to comprehend what it takes to meet and find Mr Right these days. There's no point arguing. They don't get it; the last time they dated was probably 1203 BC. It's much better for your overall sanity and happiness to agree and change the subject.

For a while I also stopped attending extended family functions; I couldn't be bothered with the gossiping and getting judged from extended family. And it always made my Dad feel bad. It hurt him when people pointed out that his daughter was still single and in her late thirties. Already I doubted my chances on a daily basis. Who needs the extra family pressure.

Managing Unsupportive Friends, Colleagues, Flatmates and Others

Friends are mainly on your side too. I say 'mainly' because the odd one here or there secretly isn't rooting for you.

If friends don't support your efforts in finding love, drop them. Dating is tough so surround yourself with supportive friends. Trying to find love isn't illegal. If they call you names such as 'desperate' because you're constantly dating, again, ignore. It really doesn't matter what they say. Don't worry because secretly they admire your tenacity. I promise, once you're happily married you won't care either. You're too happy living your life, building a home and making future plans with your husband.

If you live with a flatmate who is unsupportive or calls you names such as 'desperado' or 'gold digger'. Move out. If it's your place, give notice and ask her to leave. If you can't do any of these then here are some tips.

Don't share anything or share as little as possible. It's sometimes hard especially if she listens in on your calls despite you taking the call in your room. This is particularly annoying but, if she asks anything, say something non-descript.

Don't share any date details, neither the good nor the bad. If you share the bad, she may be sympathetic but deep down she'll be happy because it makes her feel better about her own single status. If you share the good, you'll have to deal with envy and jealousy. It's best to say very little. You're only living together in a flat-share. Do your share of the cleaning and abide by the house rules; other than that, you owe each other nothing. Another reason to say very little is in case she drops you in it when your date picks you up. You don't want her 'accidentally' saying anything like 'oh sorry, I thought you were the other guy'. Also be prepared she may hit on your date. Don't say I didn't try and warn you.

Similarly, if you have children, be careful what you share. Who knows what they may say.

Releasing the Outcome

The one thing you can't control is the outcome. While dating, release any attachment to a specific result and live in the wisdom of uncertainty. Attachment is based on fear and insecurity, while detachment is based on the unquestioning belief in the power of your true self.

Examples of trying to control the 'outcome' include some of the following:

Will he call back?
When will he call?
Does he like you?
Why hasn't he texted?
Does he want to be with you?
Will he turn up on time or will he turn up late?
Will he stand you up?
Will he book a nice restaurant?
Will he pay? What should you do if he doesn't pay?
Expecting him to treat you in a particular way.
Expecting to know ALL the date details including exact time and venue prior to accepting the date.
Getting upset if he didn't 'date' you in the way you wanted.

You can't control any of the above. All you can control are your own actions - which is hard enough.

Intend for everything to work out as it should, then let go and allow opportunities and openings to come your way. In short do your part and release the outcome.

PART FIVE
ON THE DATE

The Date Zero

Let me acquaint you with the date zero.

The date zero is the very 'first date' when meeting someone whom you met online, via an app or a blind date. It's the first face to face or real-life physical meeting. The idea is a quick drink meeting to check him out. It's a quick 'meet and greet' or 'discovery' meeting.

Marvellous invention and here's everything you need to know about the date zero.

The date zero lasts no more than two hours although it can be shorter. The idea is that you're in and out within two hours max. No messing about, no long six-hour dates, little investment in terms of time. You meet him, have a coffee or a drink, end the date first and you're outta there.

The date zero can be any day or time except Saturday evening. For example, you can have a date zero:

- Any week day (presumably) after work.

- In your lunch hour.

- Saturday morning, afternoon, or early evening. You can meet say 4 pm on a Saturday, have a quick drink, make an excuse and you're off.

- Sunday morning, afternoon or evening.

One reason for staying away from Saturday-night dates is because there are certain expectations associated with Saturday night. Come on it's Saturday night. It's harder to make an excuse after two hours, especially if he's booked a restaurant and suggests meeting for cocktails first.

That said, if you don't know how to navigate setting up a date zero (takes some practice but once you know how it's really easy.) Now you're stuck with a Saturday-night date-zero date. In this instance don't try to reverse engineer. If you've agreed to a Saturday night date zero and he's taken the trouble to make date plans, don't cancel or try to demote to a drink date only. It's much better to go. Get it over and done with already. It's only a date.

Men who want to date you ask for Saturday night dates. The date zero with my husband was on a Sunday afternoon. He originally asked for Saturday but I turned him down. I used to turn down all Saturday-evening date zeros. Many times men don't look like their profile pictures and most turn up late. A quick lunch date zero is less in terms of an investment and easier to end first. This also avoids getting stuck in a restaurant on a Saturday evening with someone whom you don't plan on ever seeing again.

Men who like you normally try to prolong the date. They're always looking for ways to spend more, not less, time with you. Even though you agreed to meet for a drink, they'll offer lunch or dinner. This is normal. I usually said 'no thank you' to a full-blown meal, especially at the date-zero stage, but would happily munch on bar snacks.

If you meet a guy at a speed-dating event or in a bar, and he asks for your number and sets up a date, that date isn't classified as a date zero date because you've already 'met' in real life. That date is a 'date one'.

Most men won't make it past the date zero. You'll have lots of date zeros. Very few men progress past the date-zero stage. If this happens to you, again this is normal and there is nothing wrong with you. Keep setting them up.

Don't invest too much at the date-zero stage; it's simply a 'discovery' meeting to get acquainted in real life. It's in your interests to keep the date zero to a quick drink. If you like each other, he can always call you for another date. And don't worry that he didn't book a fancy restaurant for the date zero. Again, there's plenty of time for fancy dates after he's passed the date zero.

Some girls won't accept a coffee date; they don't want to get all dressed up for just a coffee date. If this is you, I have two solutions for you, either plan two or three date zeros for the same day, or plan something for afterwards maybe head to a sports bar solo or join a speed-dating event. That way all your efforts to get dressed aren't wasted. Other girls won't accept a coffee date zero due to a misguided notion that they deserve more than 'a drink' for a date zero. This is a mistake and a little shallow. Many of your date zero's will go nowhere. It's in your interests to keep the date short.

Best Days for a Date

Generally speaking, Saturday nights are date nights the world over. For any fans of *The Rules* by Ellen Fein and Sherrie Schneider, *The Rule* or guidance is that the first three dates can be any day, after that he has to ask for Saturday. At the date-zero stage there's no need to hold out for a Saturday-night date and no day is inferior to another. In the beginning the aim is to meet as many men as possible before agreeing to exclusivity with any one guy.

To clarify, the first three dates can be any day which means any day of the week. Don't get hung up or offended if he asks for a Monday lunch date. This is great for anyone with a busy workload or schedule. It works to your advantage. Get the date over and done with as quickly as possible. Lunch time dates (when I could get them) were actually my favourite: quick coffee, back at my desk and a whole evening free. I could run home after work, arrive home sweaty and it didn't matter. It's not like I had to get dressed up for an evening date.

Some girls consider any day other than Saturday as inferior. They want to nail Saturday night dates from the bat. They will only accept a Saturday-night date zero or nothing. They reason that if he starts by asking for Saturday night then he must be into them. Plus, they feel they are setting precedent for Saturday-night dates. It gives them security and assurance. They 'know' he likes them enough to ask for Saturday.

I get it but try not to act from a place of insecurity. Act from a place of confidence, assurance and abundance. If he makes it past the date zero, he gets to date you on Saturday night soon enough anyway.

Don't fill up your schedule in order to force, cohere or pigeon-hole him into asking for Saturdays either. There's no need for anything like this. Men who want you, automatically ask for Saturday dates straight away. Why? He's found his dream girl. Do you know how hard that is? Think how hard it is for you to meet Mr Right. If he thinks you're his dream girl, there's no one else he'd rather spend Saturday night with.

As with everything there are a couple of exceptions, for example if either of you work Saturday nights. If he works Saturdays, he will try and rearrange his schedule. If you're serious about dating I suggest trying to do the same. If this is impossible for either of you, Friday or Sunday evening becomes your new Saturday date nights.

When scheduling your weekly diary, make sure you're available to date. Making yourself available is all about creating space in your super-busy, hectic schedule in order to date.

While men find women with full and busy lives very attractive, don't become impossible to pin down. Provided he's asking for dates and gives three days' notice, go. He can't take you out if you're never available. To turn him down repeatedly when he asks in advance and for Saturdays is crazy. If he's tried umpteen times but you're impossible to pin down, he will move on and that could be why you're single and 'she' isn't.

Confirming Date Plans

Navigating this step of the dating process has caused so many sleepless nights, confusion and angst amongst single females everywhere. This agony is normally experienced at the date-zero stage only. As stated most men won't make it past the date zero. If he makes it past the date zero and he wants you, he will start planning ahead.

To kick off, let's begin with some facts you should know and accept. None of this is made up. I experienced this personally and so have the hundreds of singles I've coached, including the many thousands coached online. If this happens to you, and it will, it's normal.

Here's a typical scenario:

Let's say you meet through a dating app. He asks for a date and you agree Saturday evening. Now it's Saturday morning and he hasn't confirmed the date plans. You don't know what time or where you're meeting, whether he's picking you up or whether you're meeting him someplace else.

Here are some facts you should know, accept and make peace with.

Fact one: It's very rare to know exact time, date and venue before agreeing to a date. As a minimum you will probably know one or two key pieces of information. Rarely the exact date plans. To decline a date until he confirms all three pieces of information for example exact time, place and venue is a big mistake. Mainly because it never happens. Sometimes it does but mostly it doesn't

There's no need to refuse a date or say anything like:

'Let's reschedule until you have all the date plans.'
Or
'Sure, let me have the date plans once you know.'
Or
'My week is busy; please confirm date plans so I can schedule accordingly.'

You, my dear reader, are a smarty cat. You already have the date details as follows.

- The day which is Saturday, right?

- You agreed 'the evening' which means the date time will be anything between 6 pm to 9 pm.

- You may not have the exact venue i.e. the Thai restaurant on the High Street. Since he comes to you, more than likely the date will take place somewhere in your neighbourhood. A date-zero drink date will take place in a local coffee shop or a local bar. Most of my dates including the date zero with my husband took place in the same place a brasserie/cafe called Del Aziz on Vanston Road, a stone's throw from Fulham Broadway Station; yours may too. I knew how to dress because my date outfits were pre-planned and already geared towards drink dates taking place in my neighbourhood.

Fact Two: Most men confirm the date plan on the actual day. They will call on the day to confirm the date. If the date is taking place for example at 6 pm, he may call at 3 pm, some call as late as 5 pm. It doesn't matter when he confirms as long as he confirms.

Some men confirm in advance although this is rare; he confirms when he confirms. Your role is to get ready as if the date is happening and don't get anxious. He really doesn't realise you're waiting for him to confirm the exact details. Telling him off for not confirming sooner or saying anything antsy like:

'You left it late.'

'I've been waiting all day for you to confirm.'

'So you finally decided to get in touch.'

'You could have confirmed sooner, now I have to get showered and changed in less than an hour.'

'I see forward planning isn't your forte.'

He will find this mildly annoying. He will think:

'Wow what?? So she's getting worked up because I didn't call earlier?'

It's a turn off for him. Telling him off is very unattractive for him. He called to confirm date plans, and he wasn't expecting to get told off.

He isn't doing it on purpose. It's the way men are wired. In his male mind he thinks:

'Well, we already agreed the date earlier this week, what's the big deal.'

Men don't realise girls like to know in advance. Men don't realise we like to plan and know ahead of the date.

Fact Three: Most men arrive without a date plan

Most men arrive without an exact date plan especially if they're travelling to you. When he arrives he may say something like:

'So what do you suggest?'

Or

'What do you recommend?'

This doesn't mean he is unable to lead, neither does it mean he isn't prepared to do the work in organising the date. He's actually trying to please you. In his male mind he thinks:

'Since this is her town, she knows more than I do. If there's someplace she likes, I'll take her there. At least I know she'll like it.'

He's only asking for a preference; he's letting you pick as a way to make you happy. The way to hand the reins back is to lead him to the main thoroughfare, stand there, and say something like

'Emmm well... there's a bar here and some coffee shops over there, emmm not sure what do you think?'

Wait until he processes the information and let him make the final decision. If he's paying, he should also get to pick.

Fact Four: Whether he confirms a week or two hours before isn't indicative of how he feels about you. Don't assume men who confirm in advance are Mr Right. Not always! Even if he confirms days in advance (which is rare) he may still cancel - and sometimes he will.

Some men are organised and others not so much. Don't falsely assume that Mr Right will always plan ahead. Not necessarily, especially at the date-zero stage. Don't focus so much on what Mr Right should and shouldn't do. Focus on how Mrs Right should and shouldn't act in any given dating situation.

On the date zero with my husband I knew the day and time. We met on a Sunday at 2 pm. He didn't have a venue. Since he travelled to me, I knew the date would take place in my neighbourhood. He asked me to pick. We drove to the main thoroughfare, I pointed out various bars and restaurants and he picked.

Here are some of the most commonly asked questions/statements around this scenario together with my responses:

Q: Don't I need all three pieces of information for example date, time and place before accepting a date?
A: No you don't. And you will rarely have all three before agreeing to a date. Knowing the date and time at this stage is enough. Get ready as if the date is happening and wait it out. Read while you wait. Some girls absolutely insist on having a time, date and exact venue before agreeing a date, otherwise they won't accept a date. They may boast that they always know the exact time, place and venue. What she doesn't realise is how many men she is actually turning off. A little less control may equal more dates.

Q: My time is precious. I'm very busy and need to know the details upfront.

A: I'm sure it is. Telling a man how to date you, doesn't work and will back-fire. It's a turn off for him. It's much better to wait it out and watch his actions. Waiting it out reveals everything you need to know and saves time in the long term. If he cancels for example, this means he's not into you. Time-saving information. One less to worry about.

Q: Can I contact him to confirm date plans?

A: No never! It shows too much interest. It's a mistake to call, check or confirm 'Whether you're still on?'

He shouldn't know that the only thing you have to look forward to is the date with him. If you're super busy and calling in order to organise your schedule, still, wait it out. If he confirms too late and now you made plans, simply turn him down. This little 'action' taken by you speaks louder than any words.

Q: I don't want to get stood up.

A: Men who confirm date plans in advance can still stand you up. I got stood up and so will you. It's annoying. Welcome to urban dating. If you're all dressed up and he stood you up, head to a singles event. Conversely head home and forget about it.

Q: How long should I give him before he confirms?

A: If you're meeting at 7 pm, give him until 6 pm and then make other plans. In my personal dating experience, the latest any guy ever confirmed for a date was 3 pm. I have one client whose date confirmed at 6 pm for a 7 pm date and it all turned out fine.

For the most part he's not doing it on purpose. Maybe he didn't confirm sooner because he was busy at work. Sometimes he may confirm in the morning. He confirms when he confirms. Normally he will call or text and say something like:

'Are we still on for tonight?'
Your response is always:
'Sure sounds great.'
Have a backup plan - which may be heading home to watch TV.

Q: If he was excited about meeting me, he would plan in advance.
A: He probably is excited and he's probably thought about where to take you. I can guarantee that your light and breezy response when he finally confirms date plans will make him gooey gaga mushy over meeting you. Men are suckers for a girl with a great attitude.

Q: Should I explain the real reason I'm turning him down is because he didn't confirm in time? This way he will know for the next time?
A: Sure but it won't serve you. It's not likely to increase his friendly feelings towards you, if anything he will think:
'Goodness so she's getting mad because I didn't confirm on time, if this makes her mad, what will happen with the big things?'

This is how his male mind works. It's much better not to verbally show annoyance. Show him with actions. If he confirmed too late, turn him down.

Remember he's looking for a committed relationship. And just like you, he wants the whole package. He doesn't want to date someone who complains whines or gets mad easily.

Every other girl out there is already acting neurotic. She won't accept a date unless she knows date plans in advance. The fact that you're 'easy, breezy' is a huge dating competitive advantage.

To confirm: at the very beginning don't worry if you don't have the exact date plans, you rarely will. Get ready as if the date is happening and wait it out.

Bookmarking

Let's talk about bookmarking.

What is bookmarking?

Let's say you meet him at a bar and he says any of the following:

- 'Maybe we could meet for a drink over the weekend?'

- 'If you're free later this week maybe we could catch a movie?'

- 'Maybe we could meet for a drink sometime?'

- 'If you're free there's a great restaurant we could try out.'

This is very different to:

- 'Are you free for a coffee Saturday afternoon?'

- 'If you're free Sunday afternoon, we could maybe meet for a drink?'

What's the difference? For the novice datee it's hard to differentiate. Men who bookmark generally don't follow up, won't travel to you and ask for last-minute dates. Don't drive yourself crazy deciphering whether he is bookmarking or asking for a genuine date. Truth be told, the realisation that you were bookmarked comes after he failed to show.

In a nutshell examples one and two are 'general' statements. Examples three and four are a little more specific, albeit marginally. There's a day and a time although not exact. We've already run through that haven't we?

By the way, whether you think he is bookmarking or not, your response is always the same which is:

'Sure sounds great.'

Don't say anything like:

'Sure let me have the details.'

No need. If he asks for a date, he knows he has to come back to you. Men really aren't stupid.

Let's run through how to handle being bookmarked. Let's say you meet at a singles meet up and swap numbers. At the event he says:

'Hey maybe we could grab coffee over the weekend if you're free?'

You respond:

'Sure sounds great.'

He texts on Saturday afternoon with 'how about that coffee?'

In this instance since you heard nothing at all, no text, no call, absolutely nothing, and since 'over the weekend' is a little ominous - it's hard to plan for 'over the weekend - tell him:

'So sorry, didn't realise we had plans; maybe another time?"

There's no need to worry. If he likes you, he'll get back in touch.

How Can I Stop Myself from Being Bookmarked?

You can't. It's a little like saying:

'I will only accept job interviews that lead to job offers.'

Trying to control whether or not the interview will lead to an actual job offer is impossible. Sometimes the job offered is already assigned to an internal candidate. Nonetheless the company have to conduct external interviews. It's a complete waste of everyone's time. They have no intention of giving you the job. Asking them upfront before agreeing to the interview is futile. They're unlikely to confess:

'Yes, Sue from sales is already earmarked for the job. We're completely wasting your time. Please attend the interview anyway, otherwise we're in breach of our HR policy and could get fined.'

You can only do your part which is agree to the interview, dress accordingly and turn up.

Fair? Unfair? That's life!

Anti-Bookmarking Techniques

Give it up. Even if planned in advance, he can still cancel. And know that anyone dating will get bookmarked. It happened to me and it will happen to you. Stop trying to control, accept this will happen and move on quick

If any girl ever tells you:

'No man ever bookmarked me. All my dates were always planned in advance.'

If she implies no man ever bookmarked her.

Three things to consider are:

1. She probably married the second guy who ever asked her out. Of course she was never bookmarked, especially if she ended up marrying her college sweetheart. Today's dating landscape is completely different. I wonder how she'd fare dating today.
2. She isn't dating much – anyone dating a ton will absolutely have the odd bookmark here and there. If you weren't bookmarked something would be wrong. Expect and accept bookmarks.
3. She's lying.

Don't get mad or feel bad for being bookmarked. Accept and move on.

The Man Leads

Dancing is like a slow dance where the man leads.

Your job is to follow his lead on everything.

Following his lead within the dating context means he makes the first move. He also picks and plans the date. Your role is to accept and show gratitude. If what he provides isn't good enough for you, by all means stop dating him. Just don't complain or tell him how to date you.

If he asks you to suggest, of course sure go ahead and suggest, he still makes the final decision.

After the date follow his lead. He is the pursuer. He does the majority of calling and date planning.

Telling a man how to date you is a huge turn off for him.

If you tell him;

'I only like fine dining and five star restaurants.'

'I'm not into casual bars. I like the finer things in life.'

'There's a great fancy new restaurant that I'd really like to try out.'

Saying anything like the above to 'get your own way' will turn him off.

At the date-zero stage, if you don't like his choice of venue, don't take it personally or get insulted. Things only get better. If he wants you he will plan nicer dates because he will want to please and impress you.

Pick Up the Phone

When dating if he calls and providing you hear the phone pick it up. Don't do any of the following:

- Don't ignore calls on purpose, if you hear the phone pick it up.

- Don't ignore calls as a way to test how he feels about you. What I mean is: don't ignore calls to see if he'll call again. This type of behaviour borders on the insecure.

- Don't stay on the phone for hours; you talk during the date.

- If the phone is next to you but you're in the middle of something which needs your immediate attention for example your cheese sauce is about to boil over, it's much better to take the call and say 'hey thanks for calling, I'm just in the middle of stuff or 'I'm a little busy maybe we could talk later'. Why? When dating, it's important to keep the momentum going.

- Don't ignore or block his calls as a way of creating 'obstacles'. He shouldn't need to call five times on the hour in order to win the fair maiden's hand. In short, don't play games.

If you genuinely miss the call or physically can't take the calls, that's slightly different. Chances are, if he's called a couple of times he will probably call again. The point is make sure your intentions are correct.

You don't need to pick up if:

- He's a buyer-beware.

- You no longer want to date him.

- You physically can't get to the phone for example you're in the bath or busy at work.

- You're in a bad mood and are likely to say something which you may regret later.

Should You Block his Number?

Only block if he's becoming a nuisance, in which case be sure to block him. Always safely first. If you've had a date and aren't sure about how you feel about him - don't block him. Sometimes men come back and next time you may feel differently. You never know.

How to Show Interest

Simply by showing up. If this sounds simple that's because it is. Here's how to show you're interested:

- Make an effort for dates. Dress accordingly, which as you know means wear clothes which flatter your figure. Don't turn up to dates in work clothes or in your gym kit.

- Turn up for the date. On some level and no matter how small showing up indicates interest.

- Show gratitude. Thank him for the date on the date. The optimum time to thank him is while ending the date. He will respond with 'my pleasure' or 'you're welcome'. This is all you need to do. There's no need to write a next-day, thank-you text.

- Agree to another date.

That's it! That's all the effort required on your part.

Don't tell him you're interested using any words. Don't say anything like:

'I really like you.'

'I'm interested.'

'I've never met anyone like you.'

'I've been waiting for someone like you all my life.'

'You've restored my faith in love.'

'You tick all my boxes.'

No need either to send him songs or any cutesy gifts as a way to express your feelings. Trust me, if you really like him he'll already know.

If he planned a great date or bought flowers or gifts, in all cases a simple 'thank you' will suffice. Don't say anything like:

'No one has ever done that for me before.'

'No one has ever treated me this way before.'

'You're the first man who has ever bought flowers.'

Even if he is, there's no need to tell him. Expressing yourself in this way is unattractive and too much pressure for him.

When dating, keep your cards close to your chest. As my husband says 'he who talks most has most to lose.'

It's better to say very little. Don't worry because, if he turns out to be Mr Right, there's every day for the rest of your life to express your feelings.

Showing Gratitude

Showing gratitude for a man's effort is like oxygen to him and has a lot to do with chemicals. Let me explain. When a man provides no matter how small and you thank him, he releases testosterone which makes him feel good. And he will inevitably want to do more of what makes him feel good.

There's no need to go overboard or gush; a simple 'thank you' as we've discussed is all that's required for example:

'Thank you for dinner.'

'Thank you for my coffee.'

'Thank you for my wine.'

In addition to thanking him at the end of the date, try to find at least one positive thing to say during the date for example:

'Great restaurant, sushi is my favourite.'

'The baristas made my coffee perfect.'

'This wine is so full bodied, my favourite.'

'The chef cooked my steak perfect.'

Showing gratitude for a man's efforts is almost like he cooked the meal himself or personally sourced the coffee beans.

If this feels unnatural get in the habit of thanking all men regardless of how small the gesture, soon showing gratitude for a man's efforts will become second nature.

If you're reading this and a little sceptical, here's a small test. There's no special equipment required and the test works like this. Next time you're on a date and you thank him. In the majority of cases he will respond with the actual words:

'My pleasure.'

Or

'You're welcome.'

That's because it really is his pleasure.

If what he offers isn't good enough for you, still find something positive to say. By all means stop dating him but don't complain. He doesn't want to date a whiner.

Flirting

There are endless books, so called flirting experts, courses and classes teaching 'how to flirt'.

I have great news for you: there's no need to learn the art of flirting, hire an expert, attend classes or sign up to any flirting courses.

There's no need to do any of the following:

- Touch any part of his body or your body to indicate interest.

- Stare into his eyes for a prolonged period of time and then stare away. (Of course, make eye contact but every day, normal eye contact, like you would at an interview or if you were talking to a guy at a party.)

- Sit close to him or lean in with your feet pointed at precisely 90 degrees.

- Tilt your head 40 degree to the left with your eyes half shut.

Dating is hard enough without having to worry about flirting trivialities which don't matter and mean nothing.

In terms of how to act on a date. It's no different to attending a job interview. Aim to make a great first impression, remember your ps and qs and leave him feeling good about himself.

Best way to flirt?

Flirt with your confidence and happiness. What this means is that 'flirting' comes naturally and from a place of exuberance, joy and an attitude of 'all is well with the world' - even if it isn't.

It's much easier if you're naturally feeling optimistic and joyful. You won't always feel like way. Some days it's a chore to get dressed and go on another date. However, if you're doing all the things you love or at least working on your passion, you're more likely to naturally exude confidence and happiness. Start finding your passion and in the meantime fake happy.

Here are a few tricks to fake happy until you make it.

- Read positive uplifting books and articles.

- Watch positive uplifting YouTube videos.

- Keep a gratitude diary.

- Repeat mantras which make you feel good.

- Exercise, eat well, drink water, get enough sleep.

- Spend time with people who make you feel good and who lift your spirits.

- Meditate.

- Create a vision board, save it on your phone or keep it somewhere accessible and look at it daily.

- Do any other activity in the world which makes you feel good.

- Keep taking action to meet men.

In short, it's in your interests to stay optimistic, positive and cheerful. For one happy people live longer.

Making Him Feel Warm

Another important part of dating is to make him feel warm about himself. And I'd like to spend a couple of minutes explaining this to you. When I say make him feel warm, I don't mean laugh at all his jokes and tell him how wonderful he is. Let's use a scenario that I use with clients which normally helps to clarify this statement.

Let's imagine you're meeting a friend; she's a good friend but you don't really see her much. You meet for a coffee and she starts complaining about how awful her boss is, how much she hates her job, how her family are driving are crazy and how she always has to clean up after her flatmates. She's having a hard time. What do you do? You don't say 'Wow, you sure are going through a bad spell, I'd hate to be you.' Chances are, you probably won't say anything hurtful; you'll try to make her feel a little better about herself, you'll probably say something soothing and kind.

Dating works in exactly the same way. In short don't say anything negative or critical to him especially not in the beginning.

Imagine going to a job interview and saying 'goodness, your offices are horrendous; there's no way I would want to work here.'

Even if their offices were horrendous and you could never envisage working there, you would NEVER verbalise this; you might think it but you'd never say it. You wouldn't take the job - but you wouldn't be rude.

In the same way, don't be rude on your date. Don't put him down and please don't tell him 'to take his tie off' or say anything mean about his choice of venue or what he decides to order.

Let him walk away thinking 'Wow she is *soo* nice', as opposed to 'no thanks I hope I never see her again.'

The Dead Zone

If you don't already know about the dead zone, it's a marvellous place. It takes place every weekend. Yes, every weekend unless you have a date, in which case the dead zone won't apply for that weekend.

Here are the main points:

- Weekend dead zone starts every Friday 6 pm and ends Sunday 6 pm.

- No date means you disappear.

- No need to check your phone or log into online dating sites or check any dating apps.

- If you have a dating phone and no scheduled date, you can safely turn the phone off and head out.

- If you have a scheduled date, keep your phone on in case he calls to confirm date plans.

- If he asks for a date and gives three days' notice, in this instance you can accept his calls and texts during the dead zone. Only reply to texts which are about setting up date plans and remember to end all calls first and after ten minutes.

If you have no dates, enjoy the rest. Turn everything off. Recuperate! The work starts again on Sunday.

The weekly dead zone is like a mini holiday or a small break from dating. Some loathe it; I loved it since it meant I didn't have to think about dating for a couple of days. Time to relax and rest.

PART SIX

THE FIRST FEW DATES AND BEYOND

Do Men Test You by Asking Trap Questions?

Generally, they don't. For the most part men are trying to find love. And most are doing the best they can just like you.

Sure you're going to get your fair share of buyers-bewares and time wasters. There's not much you can do to avoid this, except make peace and accept that it's a part of the dating process.

Mostly men don't ask questions as a way to trap or test you. If you feel he is doing that, or if you feel uncomfortable or irritated with the way the conversation is going, here are a few ways to manage the conversation:

- End the call as nicely as possible. If you feel uneasy or, if he starts getting abusive or makes comments which you're not happy with, tell him 'thanks for calling but I better get going' or 'well it was nice talking to you but I better get going.'

- Change the subject – this is a great technique. Simply change the subject by asking him a different question. It can be as simple as 'isn't the weather great at the moment?' or 'did you hear the rain last night?' Obviously pick a light and breezy subject, don't pick a heavy, contentious or controversial subject.

- Laugh and remember there's no need to answer his questions if you don't want to.

- Deflect by saying something playful like 'That's top secret' or 'I couldn't possibly say'.

- If the topic gets heavy, simply say 'I'm not comfortable talking about that right now' or say 'I barely know you, let's come back to that another day'.

If he asks an everyday question for example 'can you cook?' He isn't trying to test your cooking skills. I admit it's a stupid question. He probably thinks he's being funny. In this instance playfully say 'well... I guess I never burn toast, is that considered cooking?' and laugh. A stupid question never deserves a straight answer.

The more you laugh, the more he will be intrigued by you. Apply some common sense. If he asks how adventurous you are sexually or what you're wearing right now, that is way too much too soon. Simply end the call.

Please know that you're really in control. And you have more control than you think. Working with my fabulous clients I have come to realise that sometimes the exact same question will be viewed completely different by two different girls. One girl will find the funny and laugh while another may be mortified.

For example, if he asks 'how long have you been single?' One girl will feel he is judging her, will get offended and is convinced he is trying to be sneaky with his question while the other girl will smile sweetly and say 'That's top secret' and laugh.

Dating questions are no different to all those banal interview questions. Sometimes a potential employee may ask 'what do you do for fun?' I know I've been asked this question many times. What I do for fun has no bearing on my ability to do the job. As you know, a potential employer is merely asking questions as a way to build a picture and get to know you.

The more you date, the more you will realise that in the majority of cases men are not aliens. They're simply asking questions as a way to get to know you. Whilst you may perceive some of the questions as stupid, they're not trying to trick or test you.

Here's a little something my husband once said:

'Men are rational logical beings. We don't make decisions lightly. Finding 'The One' is serious business. It's not a case of closing our eyes and saying eenie meenie miney mo which one shall I pick. We ask questions as a way to gather information.

We don't do things on a whim or make emotive decisions. If it's important to him, he will take the time to do his background research.

If he only wants sex, he won't waste his time trying to find out about you. He will tell you what you want to hear in order to get you into bed. If a man is asking questions be flattered. The fact that he's asking questions means he's interested enough to find out more.'

Try not to get offended or annoyed with his questions. He is simply trying to get to know you.

How to Tell If he is Into You

The first way to tell if he is into you is he will want to see you. Men in love want to spend time with you. Here are other fool-proof ways to tell if he's into you. Please note, this list is universal to men regardless of their background, country of origin, culture or creed. This list is by no means exhaustive but it will give you an idea of how to tell if he wants you.

- Is he trying to see you?

- Does he ask for dates consistently every week?

- Does he ask for Saturday-night dates?

- Does he pay?

- Will he travel to you?

- Does he buy you gifts for no reason?

- Does he arrange for you to meet his family and friends?

- Does he want to spend the holidays with you?

- Does he remember your birthday?

- Does he organise something romantic for Valentine's Day?

- Did he buy you romantic gifts for Christmas?

- Did he ask to spend New Year's with you?

- Does he write poems, send you songs or cards as a way to express how he feels about you?

In a nutshell, if he's not trying to take you out, consistently and each week, he is not into you. Again apply some common sense. If he's away with work or out of town, of course he can't physically see you. In that instance he will still call or make contact in some way. To add, men make it very clear when they don't want you. They stop making contact and they stop trying to take you out.

Why he Didn't Call You Back?

There is much written about why men don't call back. I have lost count of the number of articles deciphering this predicament.

This again is very simple: he didn't call back because, for whatever reason, he's not that into you.

Here are a few reasons why he didn't call back. Again this list is by no means exhaustive but it will give you an idea.

You're Not his Look or Type

All men have a look or a *type*, it's completely biological and there's not much you can do to fight or change this evolutionary programming. If you're not his look, he won't call back. Don't worry he may not like your look but there are plenty of other men who will.

He Didn't Like Your Voice

Maybe he didn't like your voice. When it comes to dating 'voice' is really important and men in love call to literally 'hear your voice'. If he didn't like your voice he's unlikely to call back for another date. Again he may not like your voice but there are plenty who will love your voice.

Something You Said

Maybe you said 'I would never ever relocate'. Men generally take what you say at face value. Men want an easy life; they want to meet someone who feels like a vacation, not a battlefield.

If neither of you are willing to relocate and if this is a deal-breaker for him, he may not call back. He doesn't want to argue over where to live.

Maybe you specifically made a point of saying 'I'm not ready to settle down yet. I want to spend some time travelling the world'. If he's looking to settle, he probably won't call back. You told him you want to travel; he doesn't want to hinder your life-long ambitions. He doesn't want to waste your time or his own time if you have a passion for travelling and he doesn't. Aren't you better off finding someone who shares the same passion?

Not Ready for a Relationship,

He may not want anything serious.

Maybe he wants 'fun' which generally translates as sex without strings attached. In this case it's great he didn't call you back.

Out of his League

If he feels you're out of his league or if he thinks he can't provide in a way which will make you happy, he won't chase you.

Men want to make you happy, the reason he busts a gut at work or spends hours in the gym sculpting his body are all to attract you. He builds and strengthens his body so he can protect you. And he works hard in order to provide for you and his family.

If for whatever reason he feels you're out of his league, he won't call back. Why? It's too much pressure for him. He doesn't want to fall short or set himself up in this way. He will chase someone who is in his league. Great news for you. You're free to meet someone who isn't intimidated by your level of education, postcode, connections or earning potential.

How to Make Him Call Back?

You can't! All you can do is accept and move on quick.

Why This is Positive Feedback

Every time he doesn't call back, this is good if not great news. Literally praise the heavens. If you think about it: why want someone who doesn't want you? You shouldn't need to convince him of your awesomeness. If he doesn't see it, someone else will.

The fact he didn't call you back means:

- One less suitor to worry about. You know he's not 'the one' you can safely delete his name of the list.

- He isn't calling you back because he doesn't want to waste your time. Hence you're saving time. Why waste time dating someone who ultimately doesn't see you as his Mrs Right.

- Every 'no' means you're one step closer to a 'yes'. Try and reframe it in this way. When the guy you like doesn't call back, see it as a positive. Draw strength from Thomas Edison. He tried a thousand times before he made the light bulb. He didn't see each attempt as a 'failure;' he saw it as one step closer to finding the right solution. I don't know how many steps you will have to take. Some girls start dating and meet Mr Right the next week while for others it takes years and years. Your journey is your own.

What Can I Do?

Accept and move on as quickly as you can. Don't stop dating because one guy didn't call back. Instead find even more ways to meet men. Once happily married you won't care about men who never called back.

What you mustn't do under any circumstances is make the first contact. If you don't hear from him, never ever call him. You shouldn't have to remind him that you exist. If he needs reminding, he really isn't into you. When a man loves you and wants to be with you, nothing can keep him away.

Continue doing your part which is:

- Look after yourself.

- Get out there and date.

- Turn up even though you don't feel like it.

- Keep going.

- Keep the faith

- Release the outcome.

If it's meant to be, trust it will work out, otherwise move on as quickly as you can. Some girls get so frustrated and almost give up because one guy didn't call back. Don't let this be you. Reframe it as a positive, think abundance and not lack and never ever give up.

Don't Shout it from the Rooftops

In the beginning keep any new romance to yourself and I'll explain why.

It's so hard to meet someone you like. When you finally do, naturally you want to share the good news with your nearest and dearest. But relationships undergo many ebbs and flows and sometimes things won't work out in the way you want. It's in your interests to keep it quiet - at least until you know he's 'the one.' Until then resist the urge to spill the beans.

Be careful with girlfriends too. They may innocently blurt something out in the name of 'helping' you - such as 'she always had a crush on you'. As you know, not everyone (even those whom you count as your closest friends) will be happy for you. As we've run through, they're not doing it on purpose; it's more that your happiness reminds them of their single status.

If you must share, find a trusted friend. Otherwise keep it to yourself. Florence Scovel Shinn in her book *The Game of Life and How to Play It* explains that you disperse your forces by talking too much about your business. She also says that 'silence is golden'. Try to keep things to yourself, especially until you're exclusive. And don't overshare on social media. In fact, share very little and, if possible, not at all.

If your family and friends do ask how things are going, simply tell them in a nonchalant yet friendly way:

'Nothing much to report.'

Or 'yes he was ok, we'll see what happens.'

Keep it top line and don't over indulge. If you have over-shared in the past start holding back from now on.

If you live in a traditional culture or if your family is very traditional, apply extra caution, introducing different men to your family has the potential to damage your reputation. It's in your interests to safeguard your reputation. In some cultures the only man who will ever meet your family or at least your parents is the man you're going to marry. Often 'meeting the family' signifies marriage. Once he's met your family, you're pretty much heading to the altar or to the temple depending on your culture and background.

If this is your culture. Only introduce him to your family once you're serious about each other, I would advise to even wait until engagement.

Who to Take Advice From

Let's begin with who 'not' to consult for advice.

Don't take advice from any of the following types of people:

Single friends or family

No doubt you love them and, yes, they probably know you better than anyone, unless they're dating or at least trying to date, don't ask single friends and family for advice.

If they're single and not even trying to date, they have no idea how tough urban dating is. They may also mock your efforts to meet Mr Right. It's not intentional, they don't realise how much this hurts especially when you're trying hard to meet Mr Right. If they give you advice, thank them but ignore it.

Unless they were once married or are dating, don't bother asking for their advice at all. It's parallel to taking business advice from someone who has never set up a business. Sure if they've set up a business and failed, you could ask them for 'how not to do it', otherwise don't bother.

Man haters

No brainer! Don't take advice or even bother talking about your relationship with man haters. No point. Their opinions are skewed since they only see the worst in men. Yes, men can be annoying but they also bring their own unique gifts.

Bitter ex-wives with a sense of entitlement

Don't take advice from any woman who is bitter about her split or divorce. If the ex-wife or girlfriend reaches out as a thinly veiled attempt to 'warn you', take her words with a pinch of salt. Question her motives and do your own research. Again, use your judgement. If he's been convicted for wife battery stay away; otherwise take your time dating and judge him based on how he treats you.

Who to Take Advice From

Take advice from people who have what you want. Always look to see who is giving the advice. Take advice from singles who are actively dating or, as a minimum, trying to meet Mr Right. Happily married wives or at least women who are trying to make their marriage work are also a good bet.

Before considering anyone's advice, evaluate how the person is doing in his/her life. Consider the following:

- Is this person living a life that you want for yourself?

- Is the person successful in the goal that you're pursuing?

- Does this person have knowledge and expertise in what she is commenting on?

If the answers are 'no,' 'no,' and 'no,' then feel free to discount what she says.

Finding the Funny

You're not always going to want to laugh. Most days you will want to cry. And by no means am I suggesting maintaining a constant happy-clappy attitude in the face of dating adversity. I'm simply saying to look on the bright side as much as possible.

Finding Mr Right is probably one of the most important decisions you will ever make. It can take years. There will be good and bad days, mostly bad but try your best to find the funny. First and foremost, please understand in the majority of cases he's trying his best too. If his best doesn't live up to your expectations or standards, keep dating until you find someone whose 'best' is good enough for you.

If you can start seeing 'adverse appearances' as working for your good this will help you survive the dating jungle. For example, if he didn't call you back, this so-called 'adverse appearance' as we've discussed is actually good since it stops you wasting time on men who don't want you.

Also when faced with a tricky or awkward dating question or scenario try to laugh. If you're convinced that he's asking trick questions or testing you, simply laugh and say something non-descript like 'Goodness now there's a question' or say 'Great question, I'll have to come back to you'.

The girls who laugh and decide to 'find the funny' have an easier ride than someone who takes every rejection personally because it's not personal.

Dealing with Rejection

You may have heard the saying 'rejection is God's protection'.

Try to see rejection as God's or life's protection; reframing it in this way will help you move on quicker.

The path to love isn't all rah-rah moments. You're going to have your share of ups and downs. Nothing is wasted if you learned something from it. Every break-up, rejection, starting over after a divorce or relationship breakdown, comes with lessons, insights and opportunities; it's up to you to identify them. You never start over with nothing so long as you have yourself.

Surrender Your Fear of Rejection

You're the only one responsible for your dating success. And like all other aspects of life, you can increase your success rate by getting out there, enduring rejections, picking yourself back up and trying again.

Every No is a Yes

Remind yourself that 'every no is one step closer to a yes;' this will hopefully give you the strength to keep going. This doesn't mean that your next date will lead to Mr Right although of course, if it does, great. If you're going through a bad spell (and you will) update your vision board, keep repeating positive mantra's and keep taking action to meet men. Do what you must to stay positive. It does end. He will come. It happened for me and it will for you too.

Moving on from a Bad Date

As you know by now you will have your fair share of crumby dates. Men will turn up late, some will cancel, and others won't look anything like their dating profiles. Your thoughts will start playing tricks on you. You will think 'maybe I'm meant to stay single' or 'maybe it's not meant to happen for me'. You may conclude that your single status is some kind of divine payback for a past life of sin. Maybe you committed adultery in your past life and now the universe demands payback by keeping you single.

I can honestly and truthfully say these thoughts are:

- Absolutely normal. I can't recall how many single girls think like this.

- Completely false.

I don't have a magic bullet for you. After a bad date, pick yourself back up and take more action. Even if you're already subscribed to umpteen dating sites and dating apps, sign up to more singles events or join a club frequented by the type of men you want to attract.

The worst thing you can do is stop dating or take a break from dating. Don't let one or two bad dates stop your search for love. As a matter of fact, don't let a hundred bad dates stop you either. Don't stop until you find Mr Right.

Never give up

If you never give up, and keep working on yourself in the meantime, staying positive as much as you can, it will happen for you when the time is right.

If you decide to never give up you're bound to succeed. But if you believe that rejection is the end of the world, I hope you're prepared for the world to end. You can't quit, here's a great poem I shared on my blog.

Don't Quit

When things go wrong, as they sometimes will,
When the road you're trudging seems all uphill,
When the funds are low and the debts are high,
And you want to smile, but you have to sigh,
When care is pressing you down a bit,
Rest, if you must, but don't you quit.

Life is queer with its twists and turns,
As every one of us sometimes learns,
And many a failure turns about,
When he might have won had he stuck it out;
Don't give up though the pace seems slow–
You may succeed with another blow.

Often the goal is nearer than
It seems to a faint and faltering man,
Often the struggler has given up,
When he might have captured the victor's cup,
And he learned too late when the night slipped down,
How close he was to the golden crown.

Success is failure turned inside out –
The silver tint of the clouds of doubt,
And you never can tell how close you are,
It may be near when it seems so far,
So stick to the fight when you're hardest hit –
It's when things seem worst that you mustn't quit.

Author unknown

How to Handle Break-Ups and What to Do

Break-ups suck! And we've all had them. After a break-up the last thing you want to do is get dressed up and head to a singles party but that is exactly what you should do.

If you're going through a break-up, here are few ways to move on quickly:

- Delete all his correspondence including, all texts, all emails, any Facebook messages, messages via Whatsapp, any love letters, poems etc.

- Delete his number from your phone.

- If he's on your Facebook or social media put him on 'limited view;' block him or, even better, delete him. You don't have to tell him either. He doesn't need to know, no announcement required. Just do it.

- Shred or delete any pictures of the two of you together. This is no time for nostalgia. Delete them all. You have a life to live which no longer involves him.

- Bin any birthday, Valentines and Christmas cards. Read them one last time if you *really* must, after that bin the lot.

- Sell, bin or give away any gifts/presents.

- If he gave you cutesy presents like teddy bears etc, give them away to a local children's hospital or hospice. Gone. See ya. Next.

- Refrain from contacting him in any way.

- Don't answer his texts or take his calls.

- Don't respond to him crying on the phone. Don't have a weak moment and think 'oh I feel so bad he was crying on the phone and he really wants to see me'. He doesn't. Even if he does, we don't care. Remember, men who want to date you don't break up with you.

- Date IMMEDIATELY. If you're feeling the bluest you've ever felt in your whole entire life and you feel everything sucks - start dating asap.

The reason you have to bin and delete is because of a chemical called oxycontin, oxycontin is also referred to as the love or cuddle hormone. In women it's designed to keep us bonded with the male. Every time you read his sweet texts or look at his cards, you release oxycontin which makes it slower for you to move on and we want to move on quick. The quicker you move on, the more chance you have of meeting Mr Right.

Yes, you're allowed to cry and feel sorry for yourself but that shouldn't stop you dating others. When a guy breaks up with you, try and see it as a gift; he's freed you to meet someone better. In a couple of months' time or possibly sooner, you'll look back and wonder 'What. Was. I. Thinking'.

Anytime you break up with someone, you always end up meeting someone better.

PART SEVEN

ABOUT HIM

What You Want Versus
What Men Want

We're all focussed on what we want. When I talk to clients, most start the conversation with what they want. For example, they may say:

'I want a guy who is professional, successful, knows what he wants, isn't afraid to speak his mind, likes sport and enjoys travelling.'

This is great; it's good to know what you want. But what if this 'type' of guy isn't searching for someone like you?

If your complaint is 'I can't find what I'm looking for', to recap maybe what you're looking for either a) doesn't exist or b) does exist but he's not looking for *you*; he's looking for someone else. Here's the thing: as we spoke about in the beginning you have to become who you want to date.

I only have good news: the more you become who you want to date, the more men you'll attract. You won't attract every man, because not every man wants what you have to offer.

It's similar to looking for a job: often the more qualified you are in your chosen vocation; the more opportunities you have to get the job YOU want. In the same way, the more date-able you are, the more men there will be for you to either reject or accept. Isn't that a great position to be in?

In terms of what men want, as already pointed out it's all about whether you're his 'look' or his type. Men fall in love with their eyes. If you're not his look or type, he won't chase you. It's all biological and evolutionary and the way men are wired. Who wired them? Mother Nature. Getting angry is a little like getting mad with the weather for being the weather.

Men want a girl who looks after herself and has a great personality. As you know by now it's all biological. A girl who looks after herself is more likely to be healthy and healthy equals good gene-carrier. Men don't want a diva, girls who are hard work, attract drama or are high maintenance. They're not interested in them because most men want an easy life. There's enough drama in the world; he doesn't want to come home to constant drama, it's too exhausting. I've never heard a man say 'I want someone who is hard work, insecure and doesn't value herself'.

Am I suggesting anyone who wants to attract a mate should become a people-pleasing door mat? Absolutely not, because he won't respect you. If you don't think you're awesome neither will he.

A man looking for a long-term partner will categorise potential mates in two ways:

The 'for now' girl – he likes you but he won't marry you. Yes, he'll take you out and pay for dates because he knows that's what he has to do to keep you happy, but that's all.

The 'keeper' – this is the girl he will make his wife, the girl he will introduce to his family, the girl he will work hard to support, protect and provide for. This is his dream girl.

Men know straight away if you're the one. Men who want you don't need years to figure out whether you're 'the one'. He doesn't need years because he doesn't want to lose his dream girl. Men are territorial. He'll put a 'ring on it' sooner rather than later. He doesn't want another male wooing his dream girl.

That said, it all starts with you.

If you want to attract a great guy become a great girl. If you're attractive but high maintenance, yes he'll date, wine and dine, sleep with you if you let him, but he won't stick around. Do you have to be good-looking in order to attract a mate? Again, absolutely not.

Some of the world's most attractive actresses and super models are single. What is considered attractive to one male isn't necessarily attractive to another.

How can you win when biology and evolution play such a huge part in mate selection? Increase your date-ability. Look after yourself, exercise, eat well and stay positive. This way YOU get to pick the very best man for the job.

Weeding Out the Time Wasters and Undesirables

Getting your fair share of undesirables and time wasters comes with the territory.

Don't think there's anything wrong with you. It's normal. Men don't necessarily think of themselves as timewasters.

Either he's bored, looking for some 'time pass' or trying his luck. Try and accept that this will happen to you. No point complaining. Plenty of 'Mr Wrongs' will contact you. Dating is a numbers game. The trick is to recognise these types, and move on quickly.

Here are what I label as 'undesirables' together with how to weed them out.

Married Types

If you find out he's married, stop dating him. Sometimes married men will attend singles parties and balls which is a little unfair. I attended speed-dating events where the odd guy here and there turned out to be married. Some men who are online dating and using apps are also married. If you're reading this and dating a married man, stop dating him ASAP! Even if he leaves his wife for you, what he did to her he can do to you.

Gamblers

Don't bother; you don't need the drama. Dating isn't charity and don't take it on yourself to reform him.

Alcoholics/Drug Addicts/Ex-Convicts/Con Men

Think twice and stay away.

Men Who Stand You Up or Cancel a Date

If he stood you up or cancelled even once, forget about him. If he tries to organise another date, don't take his calls or respond to any of his messages. And don't listen to any lame excuses. Even if the worst thing happened, still no excuse. He could have called or texted to let you know if he couldn't make it.

Men Who Ask to Go Dutch

Stop dating any man who asks to go Dutch. If he asks to split the bill, pay your share and never see him again. There's no point accepting another date. Any man who asks to go Dutch or doesn't even buy you a drink is a next.

Men Who Ask to Meet Halfway

Men who ask to meet halfway aren't into you. For him you're a 'possibility.' He thinks you're OK but not worth the travel. Sure he'll meet you provided you travel to him. Men who want to date you, travel to you. It's their pleasure. I have countless stories where he travelled sometimes across the globe to be with her. A two or three-hour drive is nothing for a man in love, nothing at all. And he travels with a huge smile on his face because he gets to see you.

Men Who Disappear or Give Mixed Messages

If he misses a week, disappears for some time and there's no scheduled future date, treat with caution. You should always know when your next date is or he should make efforts to try and pin you down for another date. He doesn't exist unless he's trying to take you out.

Still in Love with the Ex

Move on from any man who talks about trying to get his ex back or is still in love with his ex. You don't want him; he's in love with someone else. Better he pursues her, which leaves you free to date more suitable men.

Any Men Who Forgets Your Birthday or Valentine's Day

Men who forget your birthdays or Valentine's Day are not in love with you. They like you but they're not in love with you. Stop dating him if he forgets your birthday or Valentine's Day.

He Doesn't Want to Spend the Holidays with You

Again he's not in love with you. Men in love want to spend the holidays with you. You're their most favourite person in the whole wide world and there's no one else they'd rather spend their time with. If they make excuses. Don't get upset, this is all valuable information; it frees you to meet men who are into you.

Men Who Break Up with You

If he broke up with you, he's a next. Don't wait for him to come back. Start dating others. It's not great if you're always breaking up, getting back together and breaking up. Men who want you don't break up with you.

Why?

They're too scared to lose you. What if you won't take them back or worse what if you meet someone else? If he breaks up with you, move on.

Any Man Who After a Period of Time Doesn't Introduce You to his Family and Friends

Men who see you as part of their future introduce you to their friends and families. If he doesn't bring this up or if he makes excuses for example 'family life is tough at the moment', or 'it's not the right time yet', start taking a step back. Even if his family live abroad, he'll arrange a phone or video chat so they can meet you. Rest assured he'll find a way.

Men Who Ask You to Loan Them Some Money

I think this is fairly self-explanatory.

Fantasy Relationships

Fantasy relationships are such a huge waste of precious time that they should be criminalised. Fantasy relationships include any of the following scenarios;

- The guy at the gym who keeps looking but never asks you out.

- The guy at work who always stands by your desk but never makes plans to take you out.

- The guy at the bar who keeps staring but never makes a move to talk to you.

- The married guy who looks at you. You know, just know, he would ask for a date if only he wasn't married.

- The ex who broke with you. Don't sit and fantasise about him; chances are he's moved on and so should you.

- Any man that stares, stands around by the water cooler or who happens to always join your class BUT never tries to organise a date is not into you.

Don't fantasise about these types of men. Remember the golden rule: he doesn't exist until he asks for a date.

Men Who Talk Like This

Stay away from men who say any of the following:

- 'I can't give you what you want.'

- 'I'm not into marriage.'

- 'Marriage is only a piece of paper.'

- 'I'm not looking for a serious relationship.'

- 'I'm not looking for marriage.'

- 'My parents divorced when I was two months old and it affected me profoundly.'

Men who talk like that don't want you. Don't walk, *run* away
Here are other ways to spot a time waster:

- He won't call you his girlfriend. He refers to you as a 'friend'.

- He doesn't organise dates in advance or he's missed some weeks.

- You're always the one travelling to him; he rarely comes to you.

- He won't commit to any future plans. He may talk about future plans but they never materialise.

- You don't know when you're next seeing him, in fact you haven't seen him for weeks.

- He doesn't try and include you into his life.

- His Facebook relationship status says 'interested in women'.

- You think you're exclusive yet he hasn't deleted his online dating profile.

- He is still actively using online dating sites and apps.

- He starts to moves away from you.

- He never says the words 'I Love You'.

Any man who doesn't call you back or isn't trying to date you is not into you. Nothing you do will make him into you. Your move is to stop dating him. He can only waste your time if YOU let him.

Recognising the Good Guys

Now we've worked out the so called baddies, let's focus on the good guys.

Men Who Talk About Themselves

I have read bad advice from dating 'experts' who say any man who talks about himself is a 'buyer beware' but this couldn't be further from the truth. Men talk most on the third date because they're showing you 'what they've got'. In essence they're saying 'this is me, I hope you like it.' If he talks about himself non-stop and doesn't ask much about you on the first date, this is normal and to be expected. This is actually great because if you listen you will learn so much about him, all without you saying a word or having to ask many questions. Don't ditch him because he talks about himself. Don't worry there's plenty of time for him to find out about you. Provided he is Mr Right; he has a lifetime to get to know all about you.

Men Who Don't Organise Fancy First Dates

Depending on how you met, and as already explained the first date may be a quick coffee or drink date. This is fine. He doesn't have to organise a fancy first date. I spoke to one client who was disappointed because her date organised a tapas bar for their first date. She considered this a bad sign. She felt, if he liked her he would have tried to impress with a fancy restaurant. Later I found out that he took her to his favourite tapas bar and one that he frequents often. He enjoys the food and thought she would too. Don't over analyse based on his first-date venue choice.

Men Who Turn Up Dressed Casually

The way he dresses is no reflection of how he feels about you. If he turns up to the date dressed casually, don't judge him. Maybe he has to dress formally for work and likes to dress casually in his down time. Give him a chance and don't criticise his choice of date-wear. He might not like what you wear either.

Divorced Types

Some girls who are single and never married won't consider dating divorced men. Which means more for you.

If you're divorced yourself, don't let this hold you back. Divorce isn't always a negative, especially when it allows both parties to move on and find love with someone else.

Unless you have both sides of the story, don't fixate too much on why his marriage broke down. Take your time dating and watch how he treats you. That said, apply some common sense. If his marriage broke down due to domestic abuse on his part, think twice. Don't put yourself in danger. If the marriage broke down because they grew apart or simply had nothing in common, that's a completely different story.

Men with Children

Again whether a girl will date a man with children sometimes depends on her own relationship status. Many girls who are single, never married and childless won't consider men with children because either they may not want children or they worry about the responsibility - which is understandable.

If his children are older and have fled the nest, it might be easier. They're no longer around. I'm not saying step-motherhood or blended families are easy. I'm simply suggesting you give men with children a chance. That's all - one small drink date. You don't have to progress any further. The more men you allow in, the more chances of meeting Mr Right.

If he Reschedules

If he gets in touch to reschedule the date, he gets another chance, for example if he says:

'Hey we were supposed to meet today, my client flew in from the States and I have to stay around; are you free later this week at all?'

Anything like the above, he deserves another chance. In this instance he's rescheduling, not cancelling. If he cancels but doesn't reschedule, forget about him. For example, if he says

'Hey, so sorry can we cancel today, I can't make it.'

Forget him, he's cancelled and isn't suggesting another time to meet. The two things are different; I hope you can tell the difference.

I Keep Attracting Men Who Only Want One Thing

Sorry to be the bearer of 'not quite what you want to hear' but like attracts like.

If you keep attracting the same type of man or situation again and again, I mean, if there's a pattern or if you're scratching your head thinking 'why does this keep happening to meeee?' Chances are this is something within you. Get some quiet time and try to reflect or ask a trusted friend.

Often when a girl repeatedly complains about the same situation, for example if she keeps attracting men who are overly sexual, sometimes it's the way she dresses for dates or the pictures she's posted online.

If this keeps happening to you, make sure you dress date-appropriate, which is classy and not trashy. And make sure any pictures posted on your dating sites are also appropriate. Be careful not to show off too much cleavage or post pictures posing in a string bikini holding a huge magnum of champagne - type-thing.

You may feel posing in a bikini while lounging on a sun stroller reflects your fun and playful side, unfortunately men will translate this as a 'good time girl'. It's incredible how the male mind works. Mind boggling at times but there we have it.

We always seem to think there's something wrong with the other person when in reality the work is always with ourselves. If the same scenarios keep playing out over and over, begin the search for answers by looking within.

You Get What You Focus On

I'm sure you've heard this expression aplenty.

What you think about and talk about is what you attract. If you keep focusing on what you don't want, guess what happens?

You attract more of what you don't want.

As humans we focus on the negative because our brains are more likely to retain negative information. It's a survival instinct since it stops us from getting hurt repeatedly by the same things. But constantly focusing on what you don't want means you start to attract more of what you don't want.

Here are a few things you can do while you wait for Mr Right to find you:

- Focus on the good. This doesn't mean bury your head in the sand after each and every bad date. It means move on quickly after a bad date and don't talk about it. I know first-hand how hard this can be. Especially when you're trying so hard to date and still can't meet anyone you like. It gets frustrating and you start focusing on why you're still single. You feel like you've been searching for everrrr!

- Don't talk about any bad dates; remember, they're inevitable and you will have your fair share. If you didn't, something would be wrong. The more you talk about bad dates, the more you will attract similar bad dates. I ban my clients from talking about or sharing bad-date experiences. They're not allowed to share stories via any social-media channels either.

They have to either keep it to themselves or talk with one or two trusted friends only. I would encourage you to try to do the same.

- Meditate.

- Talk to people or focus your attention on people who have what you want.

- Don't badmouth men. You can't expect to attract a great guy if you're forever bad mouthing the male species.

- Repeat positive mantras, repeat as many times as necessary.

- Exercise nearly always worked for me. It may or may not work for you. Find what works for you and try and stay positive. I know it's tough but it's only temporary.

Testing Men

You don't need to 'test' men or set up any elaborate schemes as a way to test him. Don't waste your energy. Stand back and watch because he will reveal himself to you soon enough anyway. Either he wants you or he doesn't. All will be revealed by his actions.

The only so-called 'test' that requires your attention is whether he loves you and whether you love him. Does he want to be with you, build a future and a life together and vice versa?

Let's run through what I mean by testing and why there's no need to bother.

Testing his feelings for you

This one is simple. Either he's trying to take you out or he isn't. That's it; there are only those two scenarios. Any other scenario for example 'it's complicated' or he's giving mixed signals or he's shy, all mean that he doesn't want you. Don't break up or punish him as a way to test how he feels about you either. Don't 'test' the relationship in this way. It may backfire. His actions will reveal exactly how he feels about you.

Ignoring calls/texts/emails/messages deliberately to test his feelings

This is wholly unnecessary and when a girl does this, it demonstrates insecurity. Some girls will purposely ignore messages and phone calls as a way to test his interest levels. They think that if he calls twice or doubles messages this is a good sign since surely it means he really likes them. Don't waste your time on these types of antics. Instead use the time to exercise, try out a new recipe or catch up with a friend. Don't miss his calls or messages on purpose either, as you already know don't play games.

Setting him up

Don't set him up to test how he handles himself in a particular situation. For example waiting by the car door to test whether he'll open it or offering to pay to test whether he'll decline the offer. Simply don't offer to pay and you don't need him to open the car open. Don't conduct silly tests. They may backfire and then you only have yourself to blame, sorry! Don't sweat the small stuff. Focus on the bigger picture.

Not ALL Men Are the Enemy

Bashing men and thinking 'men are the enemy' only serves to hold back your good.

Why?

You can't bash men, consider them the enemy, man-hate and expect to meet a great guy. There are single girls who constantly bash men; all they see is the bad. They feel that all men are trying to test and manipulate them and are only interested in one thing which is sex. They're continually on guard and primarily focussed on weeding out these types of men and wonder why they can't meet Mr Great.

If you think ALL men are liars, cheaters and abusers, that's what you'll attract. If your attention is focussed on looking for signs that he's a 'buyer-beware', again, you will find plenty. If you believe no good men exist, then they don't.

One of my husband's single friends recently said 'all women are liars and time wasters, most look nothing like their profile pictures'. I remember once complaining about the same thing. Finding 'the one' is serious business. Men who are looking for a serious relationship struggle just as much as women. Work on becoming Mrs Right and you're more likely to attract Mr Right.

Men find happy women very attractive. This doesn't mean you have to be happy 24/7. It means try your best to take the good with the bad. Don't let the 'bad' get you down. Of course, feel free to fake happy if you must.

Try to shift your mind-set. The sooner you make the shift the more chances you have of meeting Mr Right. The other thing to note is that if you're continually negative about men, men will pick this up and won't want to date you. Why would they? Firstly, they will find your negativity exhausting and draining. No one wants to date a moaner or complainer. Jeez what fun right? And secondly no man wants to date a man-hater. It's like dating men who hate women, why bother.

Don't instantly prejudge men for the silly things they write either. They're only trying to get to know you. Don't call him dumb or an idiot just because he didn't ask you out immediately. Don't judge him based on a single date which you perceived as 'bad'.

Think 'Law of Attraction'. If you think there are good men out there whom you will find attractive, then you will. I'm not saying be naïve and give all men a chance no matter what; I'm saying, don't bash all men so that you end up giving no one a chance.

While dating you will only ever encounter three types of men as follows:

- Those that move towards you.

- Those that move away from you.

- Those that are indifferent.

We're only interested in type one: men who move towards you. This principle can be applied to loved ones, family and friends. Any love interests that fall into type two or three - forget about them.

Look to see who is moving towards you. Is there anyone who is always hovering around, trying to get your attention, offering to fix things for you? If so give him another look. He could be Mr Right.

Why Men Are Great

Of course not all men are the same.

And yes, there are the cheaters, abusers, gamblers, alcoholics, fraudsters and drug addicts. All of these types should be avoided; you have my full permission to stay away from these types of men. But before we demonise men as the enemy, remember women are guilty of these crimes too.

Sure men can annoy us but they also bring their own unique gifts.

Here are a few of these gifts:

- Men in love are amazing, when a man wants a woman there is nothing he won't do for her. If she needs something he'll get it, if something is broken, he'll either fix it or get it fixed.

- All he wants is to love, protect, provide and support you.

- When you respect him, he will reciprocate by cherishing you.

- Your safety is of the utmost important to him.

- Men move mountains to be with the one they love.

- Men bust a gut at work for you. He works hard in order to provide for you and his family.

- All he wants is to put a smile of your face. That's it. He wants the chance to make you happy. When you're smiling he's smiling.

- They are great problem solvers.

Remember Mr Right is not in charge of your happiness; that's your job. Mr Right is simply the cherry on top. It goes without saying that women are amazing too. In fact, we run the world. Again you already know that too.

Some Truisms, Facts, Bits and Bobs in Case You Missed Them the First Time.

On Modern Urban Dating.

- Dating is hard work, exhausting and soul destroying but don't let that defeat you.

- Everyone should multiple date.

- Yes, he will call, providing he's interested in the first place.

- Men who want you don't let a missed call, text or email get in the way. They will always find a way to track you down.

- Prepare yourself for dates like you would for an interview. Organise your date outfits and practise answers to all those dating questions.

- The more you date, the easier it becomes.

- Most dates don't make it past the first date – accept it, it's the truth.

- No date is a bad date. At the most basic level you've met another human being and practised your date game.

- Some days all you want to do is scream and shout, take down your profile and cancel all your subscriptions. However, giving up is not an option.

- There are times when you seriously want to bash men across their heads with your bag. The only restraining factor is the possible damage this may cause to your bag.

- Never settle.

- Become who you want to date.

- Men will ask you to pay. Accept it and don't blow a casket because a guy who never plans on seeing you again asked to split the bill.

- Things never to do on a date:
  Take pets
  Invite friends
  Lie about vital stats
  Talk sex
  Get drunk
  Invite him back to your place

- Five deal breakers which in the real world are NOT deal breakers:
  Men who are late
  Divorced men
  Men with children
  Men who talk about themselves
  Men who profess their feelings early on– very normal

On Men.

- Most men are late for dates. Waiting for dates allows plenty of reading time. Now is a very good time to invest in an e-reader.

- Most men arrive without a plan and look nothing like their profile pictures.

- Men know to pay for dates; your role is to gracefully receive.

- Men seem to love LOL and emoticons.

- A good man is very hard to find, however they do exist.

On Digital Dating.

- Dating online and via apps works but truly sucks. Let the suckage begin.

- The profile name and written profile reveals plenty about your date. Simply read, listen and take notes.

- Everyone should post a profile picture. Preferably one that is current and recent.

- Online dating sites are full of time wasters and other unsuitable potentials. Winks, waves or being added as a favourite mean absolutely nothing. Ignore. Only invest time and energy in men who have taken the time to read your profile and write a note.

On Finding Love

- You're not alone. Love is out there, but you have to be patient and recognize it. It might not always come in the package you expect it to come in, but you'll know it when you have it.

- Mr Right only comes a few times in a lifetime hence why you will have many dates which go nowhere. Imagine, if they were all Mr Right, you'd never make a choice.

- He won't find you if you never go out and refuse to date.

- The person who wants to get ahead at work will naturally spend more time networking and investing in extra courses. Same with dating. You want to meet Mr Right, join as many dating sites and apps and get out as often as you can.

- You don't have to wait for an 'intense connection' before agreeing to a date. Chance are if you do, you will probably stay single. Stack the love odds in your favour by giving men a chance. It's only a date.

- Judge less, don't over analysis and keep an open mind. You just never know.

About India Kang

India Kang is a dating and relationship coach for women and Relationship Expert for Match UK. She is a *Rules* certified coach, *Rules* being the cult dating manual by the *New York Times* best-selling authors Ellen Fein and Sherrie Schneider.

Her first book *Why Men Ask Dumb Dating Questions* sold in nine countries, her blog is read in twenty-four countries. She is regularly featured in the press and media, and also writes an advice column.

India comes from a classic advertising background. She has worked for many of the top ten global advertising agencies on campaigns for some of the world's most recognisable brands

India is married and lives in Solihull.